ABOVE and BEYOND EXCELLENCE in EDUCATION

HARRIET GOLDIN

ISBN: 1-4392-7016-3
EAN13: 9781439270165

Contents

Introduction

It's a new dawn. Inspiration fills the 21st century with hope. More citizens are exercising their voting rights and responsibilities. People are energized and looking to a future of opportunity and possibility. They want to re-engage. To use the words of educators, who are the primary audience of *Above and Beyond: Excellence in Education*, we are in a "state of readiness" to learn, to think about community, to talk about leadership, to honor excellence. In the schoolhouses of America, there's also good news. Let's use the momentum of the teachable moment to capitalize on our strengths, tackle our weaknesses, and harness the talents of the unsung heroes in our schools who work with our nation's youth. *Above and Beyond: Excellence in Education* provides a vehicle for sharing some projects and perspectives of educators recognized for excellence by their peers that may be helpful for teachers-in-training, new teachers, veteran teachers who are looking for new stimuli, and parent-teacher groups. For those who have had the wonderful experience of connecting with exceptional teachers, *Above and Beyond* may stir up some wonderful memories as we celebrate their achievements.

> *Educators play a significant role in developing the flexibility, adaptation, and innovation needed to sustain our democratic society. They are in a unique position to help young people explore their full range of potential. Educators teach more than skills. They instill values and encourage children to be creative, curious, caring and sensitive individuals.*

(John W. Gardner, *Excellence* and *Self-Renewal*)

Often, the work that goes on in our schools is taken for granted. Newspapers and other mass media focus on the negative events surrounding students, teachers, and education policies. Ask any person in a community about what really matters and needs change; "education" is usually cited as a main concern. Yes, there are many problems in America's schools, including kids who come to school unfed, unmotivated, and lacking the basic requirements necessary to learn; unfunded mandates; and unpreparedness of the future workforce. But there are educators in every type of setting—urban, rural, suburban—and at every grade level (K-12), who are catalysts for change, making significant differences for students, affecting the quality of their lives and preparing them for a better tomorrow. Daily, these educators perform the art of teaching, listening and loving, modeling, disseminating and managing, and maintaining high expectations.

Educators—whom I define as all individuals with whom students come into contact, be they classroom teachers, administrators, counselors, nurses, special needs teachers, performing arts teachers, teachers' aides, or community volunteers—are essential to the well-being of our society. They are but some of the constituency groups responsible for connecting with children on a daily basis. And yet, the concentrated time block of five or more hours, in which an educator assumes the major leadership role, is key to children's values, attitudes, social and emotional well-being, and knowledge. Whether it is by direct articulation or modeling, educators establish an environment where children can learn with and from one another. Teachers and others in the schoolhouse complement what parents and others in the community convey about respect, being a contributing member of society, and not least in importance, knowledge and how the world works.

What appears as a broad sweep of stories of K-12 educators is a re-articulation of important themes found across disciplines, across grade levels, and in communities across America. Each of the compelling narratives elucidates a number of themes such as: *Power of Communication, Special Learners, Civic Education, Leadership, Community, Instruction, Creative Problem Solving, Professional Development, and Self-Renewal.*

My purpose for this book is to relate the stories of selected educators, their backgrounds and specific projects and processes for which they were nominated and awarded. In their own words, they express their interests, experiences, and visions for the future of education. These educators represent a huge cadre of people who really connect with students in meaningful ways. There are, in fact, many more who have been recognized for excellence by our small foundation and other local, state, and national groups. I propose to have a conversation with the readers, to share with you some exemplary practices as well as my reflections about education, which I have gained over many years. Throughout your reading of the book, I invite you to engage with me and others to revisit some ideas and issues that have emerged in classrooms and schools, debate what you feel is important, and consider solutions to some of the vexing problems we face at the beginning of the 21st century.

As you read, you might pause and reflect, "What? So what? Now what?" You might even think about how you would write your own chapter, "Reflections of the Reader." In addition to your self-reflection, I encourage you to continue the dialog with other educators, a practice that is both collegial and informative. This dialog is appropriate for a college classroom, a grade level or department meeting, a chat with a colleague or mentor, or an open discussion at a parent or community organization meeting.

There are no "shoulds" or "musts;" rather, there are "cans" and "mights." You can choose to adapt or replicate an idea based on your own interests, talents, and worldviews; you need to find what works best for you. There is a plethora of information about strategies and best practices. This book is not intended as a body of research or a philosophical treatise. Its thematic format includes my introductory comments, which are based on my own observations and experiences. Many of the themes cross over from one chapter to the next, much like good interdisciplinary teaching. Creative and engaging enrichment activities are incorporated within most of the chapters. I've included thoughts taken from my collection of "L'il Wisdoms," articles and notes saved from writers, speakers, and artists, who have made impressions on my way of thinking about education. The educators who are featured add their own "L'il Wisdoms," nuggets of collected expertise that may act as reminders that you can use and that may serve to inspire you with new ideas for your professional development. Their stories might just remind you why you went into teaching.

Validation plays an important role. Taking the time to reflect and recognize the work of a peer, subordinate, even a superior, is key. Doing so leads to good and improved performance and increased motivation. "Thank you" are words that are too often assumed and unspoken. Many of us have been touched by a teacher or someone in the community or workplace who was in a teaching or mentor role, who really saw us, listened to the stated and the unstated, and encouraged and inspired us to be all that we could be. Being noticed, complimented, encouraged, inspired, and rewarded, in some way, encourages continued behavior. Our small family foundation decided to focus on supporting the recognition and reward of educators who truly make outstanding contributions in their classrooms, schools, and communities. Validated for their efforts and achievements, these educators of excellence typically act as catalysts for other educators by sharing their projects and insights. This is evidenced during the annual celebratory experience of a regional Educators Forum, participation in an Educators Network dedicated to professional development, and through much publicity. In a very public manner, the foundation fosters the respect for and appreciation of educators. Validation helps to retain quality educators while attracting others to the profession.

Above and Beyond: Excellence in Education suggests that success is within our reach, and the charge of educators is to ignite that spark. By illuminating some "lights" of the profession, I hope to inspire many more educators and provide a sense of potential. I highlight twenty and spotlight others who commit their passion, time and energy, and make knowledge meaningfully bright for children. They are among the more than two hundred distinguished educators who have been recognized for excellence since the foundation's inception in 1990. Their accomplishments and stories have been written with the help of their nominators for the Goldin Foundation Excellence in Education awards, Advisory Board members who introduce them at the Educators Forums, and the award recipients themselves, whose words are in italics. Their light is enduring and shared by all who, through their commitment, create the ability for all learners to generate their own rays of excellence.

∽

Acknowledgements

"The mind is not a vessel to be filled, but a fire to be ignited."
Plutarch

I continue to be nourished by the many educators whom I have come to know and admire as illuminators, igniters, and visionaries. They spark the imagination of young people and provide insight to the mysteries of the unknown, while they help their students develop their potential. Daily they continue to connect meaningfully with children. They create a fantastic ripple effect that goes beyond the walls of the classroom. They are the ultimate dream builders and are valuable to our society. I sincerely thank them for their dedication and friendship.

Thank you to the many award recipients of the Goldin Foundation for Excellence in Education who devote themselves to its mission and serve voluntarily on its advisory boards, share their *Above and Beyond* stories, and foster excellence in our schools. Special thanks to my editor, Gail Duffy, a Goldin Foundation recipient and English Department Chair at Medfield High School, who, with humor and encouragement helped me clarify my writing and thinking. Carol Ziemian, another Goldin Foundation recipient, provided an initial review and encouragement. Friends and family gave continued support and inspiration. Kudos to all of them!

I am proud to be a player in this most wonderful of professions!

☙

Rays of Sunshine: A Time of Wonder, Curiosity, and Creativity

Childhood evokes wonderful memories of a time to explore, create magic, and reinvent. It's a time to just poke around and see what's under the rock, look at the intricate spider web, feel the fuzzy caterpillar, and stomp in rain puddles. All is fresh. Everything and anything is possible.

In *The Sense of Wonder*, Rachel Carson states, "A child's world is fresh and beautiful, full of wonder and excitement." She suggests that for many of us, the clear-eyed vision and true instinct for what is beautiful and awe-inspiring is often dimmed or even lost before we reach adulthood. Carson asks that our gift to each child in the world "be a sense of wonder so indestructible it would last throughout life, as an unfailing antidote against the boredom and disenchantments of later years, the sterile preoccupation with things that are artificial, and the alienation from the sources of our strength."

Too often, as students move through the school system's lock-step machine, accumulation of unrelated facts replaces Carson's embrace of childhood wonder. Why is that? How might they remain open to new discoveries and challenges, loving a life filled with experimentation? Sadly, once children enter middle school, around the age of eleven, a lot of the sparkle, creativity, and excitement for learning fade. Is that because parents become less involved in the schools? Is it because teenagers become too concerned with conforming to the demands and expectations of their peers? Is it because the "brain has taken a little time off" in its growing process, as some researchers suggest? Or, is it that we stop validating wonder as an authentic conduit to knowing?

Yet many educators continue to kindle the magical lights of wonder and discovery. They invite questions of what students do inside and outside of the classroom. Unwilling to give up on children, they overlook the research, the hormonal changes typical of teenagers, and peer pressure. The following three teachers at three different levels cultivate wonder. They leave lasting legacies.

∽

Beth Altchek, 2006

This magical teacher uses wonder as a springboard to knowing and takes first and second graders to new heights.

Beth Altchek, a combination grades 1- 2 teacher at the Lilja School in Natick, MA, is a fairy godmother. Her little charges expectantly await the start of each school day to begin their journeys of discovery. They are eager and ready to learn. Few expect children in grades 1 and 2 to reach such high performance levels in academic content and emotional and social engagement. This is due to Beth's keen intellect, tremendous creativity, and the incredible energy she generates daily.

> *I believe in bringing enthusiasm to my class. Whether it's taking themes that kids love, involving them in tackling an everyday problem such as how to remove a huge rock from a backyard, or exposing them to writing poetry, I feel it important to nourish a sense of excitement and creativity.*

> *We do have student outcomes that we must meet as defined by our school system and the Massachusetts Frameworks. Yet, we can make choices for our curriculum, and I believe that we can design activities that are fun, enriching, and challenging while meeting the standards. This was Harry Potter Year, and the children were organized in tables around the "Heads of House" with the theme extending to curriculum areas. For each of the two years that my teaching partner and I have our children in the grade 1-2 classrooms, we have three major long-term studies that last for about six to eight weeks. This year it was "Nursery Rhymes," "Simple Machines," and "Ancient Greece." There is integration of content and skills in all areas of the curriculum from math to art.*

The children have expectations that we will be doing additional "fantastic" things every year. The Poetry Café is the culmination of a project where each child writes a poem and presents it in front of thirty-nine kids and their parents in the Music Room. They have learned about elements of poetry. They have practiced their skills of oral presentation by using drama, adding more emphasis, and enunciating more clearly. For the new "Bird Guide" that we are writing, children are learning to attend to fine details, draw their own pictures, and write about their observations. With parent volunteers, they are going to the library to do research and learn about how to use reference materials and how not to plagiarize.

Beth is a community builder. She has the ability to deal with children where they're "at" with tremendous insight and articulation. She conveys to her students how unique and valuable they individually are and also how important they are to the group. Whatever the child's personality and needs are, Beth connects with each one. She deals with children by being very clear, direct, comforting, and unusually respectful. When her students share concerns from their "issues box," behaviors that were breaking down the group's sense of cooperation and community that week, there's not only a mention of them, but also an in-depth discussion occurs about the hows and whys of the ways individual behaviors affect the group, and why the children should all care.

Kids can solve problems. They have great ideas and voices that should be encouraged as they are guided to become independent decision makers. Teachers in our school have been trained in "Open Circle," a program developed by Wellesley College, that encourages kids to realize on their own about how they feel, look at specific incidences and cite the reasons/evidence, and articulate their concerns, needs, and wants. Our goal, after all, is to get children to be better human beings. It's really interesting that recently students on their own decided to develop a "happy box" in addition to the "issues box," so children can add their notes about "I'm happy because..." to be used as focus points for discussion.

Beth not only expects, but also demands, a high level of respect, equality, and support in the classroom, where she establishes a safe place for every child to take more personal risks throughout the year. Whether it's a shy child writing and performing a poem in front of the class, a struggling student who knows the class will be patient while he tries to answer a difficult math question, or a particularly inventive student who is showing the class the simple machine she spent days creating, Beth always finds time for each child to share, grow personally, and be supported and respected by his or her peers. Every student gains confidence as she finds his unique strength, one who may become the "class expert" on something or someone others can turn to for help. While a second grader might help a first grader with reading, a first grader might assist the same second grader with threading a loom during the Native American Studies unit. Children's various learning styles and strengths are addressed by the "multiple intelligence" stations in her units of study. Every child is able to find success and personal expertise somewhere through the wide variety of materials and opportunities for learning.

Beth helped initiate and implement multi-age classrooms at Lilja, which have proved highly successful.

I love teaching the grades 1-2 combination. There is power in everyone not being the same age. Having a longer period of working with children who are really

*engaged in their social, emotional and academic prog-
ress with very little downtime after the summer break is
great. While there may be differences in their abilities,
in my class there is full recognition of different talents.
Children know "this one is good at math"; "this one's
good at reading." With these strategies, few look over
their shoulders and worry about achievement. There is
genuine acceptance. The younger children stretch when
exposed to higher levels of critical thinking, for example; and by the second year, as kids know how things
work in the classroom, every child becomes a leader.
I've seen the multi-age combination work at other levels, although I'm not keen on K-1 as the needs are too
different. My bias is for the grades 1-2 interaction.*

*I'm very fortunate to have a teaching partner who is
also teaching a multi-age 1-2 class. Kristen and I have
been collaborating for many years and we capitalize
on each other's strengths. I love the synergy for program planning and implementation and recommend
that teachers, new and veteran, find a colleague with
whom they can connect and collaborate.*

Finding and addressing teachable moments are a constant in Beth's
classroom. Children are prompted not simply to answer a question,
but to ask more questions in the process of finding an answer. In Ms.
Altchek's "Math Court," these first and second grade "lawyers" present evidence to Judge Altchek about why a shape is a rectangle or
whether or not order matters in addition. One witnesses highly engaged students developing their mathematical understandings, learning to think logically, and increasing their communication skills. They
are propelled into a deeper process of critical thinking in a way that
they feel empowered as six-, seven-, and eight-year-olds. These children wonder. They question. They engage.

In her class, learning is an adventure, and creativity is a hallmark. Multiple topics and experiences become "happenings," be it Beth's travels or inviting guest speakers to the class to share their expertise. On any given day, students might see and understand the need to preserve our national parks; they might learn about the challenges of climbing a mountain in India; or they might meet a local expert on birds of prey. Lessons may include disassembly of old computers and appliances to understand simple machines or nature walks in the local town forest that lead to the building of Native American houses with children using natural materials. Beth's students delight in their own sense of wonder and excitement about discovery.

One very special series of experiences occurred when a naturalist/artist guest speaker visited her class. During their monthly walks in the woods, students observed, recorded, and sketched the day's findings, such as animal tracks and habitats. Thus, the seasonal changes of trees, identification of insect life, factors of animal habitats, and mammal signs were recorded by each student and shared with the class. Parent volunteers helped in the experiences. This series of activities led to the production of a book called *Mammal Guide*, written and illustrated by her students, which is sold in local stores, with proceeds benefitting the World Wildlife Federation. This impressive forty-page booklet is now used in other classrooms in Natick during their mammal studies.

> *I don't know if I could achieve all of my goals without tremendous parent support. Our school encourages parent volunteerism; and I have capitalized on their talents, initiative, and creativity in bringing enrichment to our classroom. Why, I even have people coming in long after their children have "graduated" from elementary school. Typically, as we embark on one of our major themes, we send an email to all of our parents telling them "this is what we want to do," and "this is what we need." For example, in Greek studies, one parent made twenty to-*

gas for our culminating Olympics. For the unit on simple machines, an engineer brought blueprints for a bridge and introduced youngsters to the scientific concepts as well as the fact that lots of different people handled the project. For our bird study, one volunteer is serving as our editor, helping us to publish our "Bird Guide," a resource book that is an outgrowth of our "Mammal Guide." For another parent it may be an offer to make plastic covers for our studies or help out with one of our many culminating events during the year. Parents know they are welcome to give whatever they can, when and if they can. Once they have participated, we recognize them. Whether it's a personal note from the teachers and/or individual notes from our students, parents and other volunteers are validated for their efforts.

Beth's impact also reaches beyond the confines of her classroom as she shares her expertise with other professionals. She was selected by TERC, a non-profit education research and development organization dedicated to improving math, science, and technology teaching and learning, to participate in a three-year study of math education in the classroom. This involved piloting new materials, contributing to curriculum development, and offering professional development. Beth has also provided graduate level courses focused on the balanced literacy model for Natick teachers, which have been very well received.

I think it is important to maintain our intellectual curiosity. As teachers, we can be learners, and there are a myriad of opportunities to keep fresh and current in our thinking and teaching. A recent professional development program piqued my curiosity and has truly impacted my teaching. "VTS" or "Visual Thinking Strategies" is a course given at the Museum of Fine Arts in Boston, which trains participants to look at an image, a painting, for example; take time, a full minute, which is almost uncomfortable to be still and look at one thing; and relate what you see and what's going on while giving evidence for your thinking. Then there is an exchange of ideas often leading to a piggyback effect as the learners hear from each other and build on the thinking.

I've used the VTS strategy in my classroom, and kids have become more perceptive in their critical thinking as they compare, contrast, and evaluate while giving evidence to support their views. I saw this recently during our Greek study when students were shown a photo of a red and black vase and came up with many perceptive thoughts. Our two grade 1-2 classes will go on a field trip to the Museum of Fine Arts in Boston, where we will be looking at paintings and sculpture and other artifacts that tie in with the curricula that we've studied, from still lives of birds to a portrait of Paul Revere to Greek and Roman artifacts. And we will use "VTS!"

For Beth Altchek teaching is more than an occupation. It is a calling.

I think one must "own" teaching before stepping into it. You do it because you're passionate about working with kids. It's a lot more than finding a job that gives you holiday and summer vacations. Loving the grade level you teach is really important. Finding the right environment that matches your criteria and philosophy is also important. I really think that if at all possible, teachers should go beyond the initial interview and "interview the building," and talk with others about the school climate, leadership, teacher collaborative efforts, and professional development. Yes, teaching may

*be tiring when one gives it her all, but it is so fulfilling!
Even when I take time to recharge, which I think is very
important to do, I'm always reflecting on my practice,
collecting things for my future projects, or considering
new ways of approaching subjects. I love making connections.*

෬

Lanie Higgins, 2007

A kinetic force, this middle school teacher's "Cool Science Incorporated" engages middle school students.

Think of a light and energy source giving off megawatts of wonder and discovery. Elaine Higgins, a grade 6 science teacher at the McCall Middle School in Winchester, Massachusetts, knows how to invest and engage kids as they learn about science, their world, and their own learning. Whether it's a CSI experience (Cool Science Investigation), a summer X2 Extreme Excellence Program for incoming sixth graders, or bringing retired scientists into her classroom to work regularly with students, "Lanie" creates excitement and motivation for learning. In her classroom, students don't simply read about the content of science. Lanie crafts experiences and experiments that actively engage her students in a wide variety of "hands on" activities, as she believes students learn by doing. This is done while combining the best of teaching practices, from multicultural perspectives to multiple intelligences, from inclusive to constructive to differentiated methodologies, so that each student can fulfill his/her potential. "Kids always come first," she says. Lanie is their best advocate, mentor, coach, and facilitator.

During any lesson there may be as many as five different activities going on, each tailored to meet the needs of various students. Every student is set up to find success in Lanie's class.

> *I liken my classroom to a restaurant where there are different menus according to whether a student is diabetic, a vegetarian, or allergic to certain foods. Teachers need a variety of things to offer, so that all students can enjoy the feast. I feel strongly that I allow for different assignments, tests, and labs. We might all be learning about "density," but I give students op-*

tions and provide flexible groupings. "Some of you like working more with math formulas, so here are special worksheets for you. Some of you like to read and want more information, so here are some suggestions for getting more material and trying some hands-on activities. Some of you prefer to do hands-on," and an aide or I will work with this group. And there's always a challenge question for those who want to pursue it. Everyone in the class will understand "density" according to his/her own strength.

I've come to realize that not everyone sees the world through my glasses. I, too, have my own learning style, and when I do a lesson, I likely present it according to my strength. But I am taking more risks, and kids are encouraged to that too. They know it's OK to make mistakes. It's OK for me to say, "I don't really like the way this experiment went. Let's try it another way." I think it important for kids to know that I and they don't have all the answers. This gives validation to their thoughts and questions and helps us navigate next steps. I used to panic about not knowing everything, but now I can say, "I don't know. That's a great question. Let's go to the Internet." I'd rather go a little slower before moving on as I think it important for students to understand the subject better. We take time to reflect by writing and discussion or sharing in small groups.

The glow of learning is a constant in Lanie's room. Kids are having fun! One lesson designed to measure "speed as a rate" uses different toys to see which will be the fastest. Students work in teams to time the wind-back toys brought in by the students. Kids love having their own toys to test and comparing them to those of their friends. They measure the distance while timing the toy in three different trials to determine an average, record their findings, and compare and contrast them. All information is recorded in their science journals.

CSI: Cool Science Incorporated is a very popular and well-attended program that was started by the assistant superintendent who wanted the district to have a science camp during the summer for eight- to twelve-year-olds. Lanie and several teachers took on this project. They worked on different curricula and tried various activities for a couple of years, some successful and some less so until Lanie thought, "Why don't I create my own curriculum?" Building upon the popular TV theme, "CSI" (Crime Scene Investigation), she developed a model that closely aligns with the Massachusetts Curriculum Frameworks and the Winchester Content Standards. It fully engages students as investigative detectives.

> *No one has done a crime scene investigation, let alone for a week. We got former students to help with the plot, and teachers generated a lot of ideas. Then we took it to a real life level. Students went to a hairdressing salon, where we had set up the scene of a robbery. A policeman came, who spent the day with us. Students also interrogated the staff. They had to assess the evidence from foot impressions, to teeth marks on pizza, dirt samples, and blood spots and come up with suspects, and later the perpetrator.*

> *The program was expanded to include a second week, each day having a different mystery such as "Mystery of Motion," "Mystery of Flight," and "Mystery of Groovy Science." These were facilitated both by experts from the community and field trips. One example involved looking at creating energy from phragmites, tall grass that is taking over swamps; and we went on a boat ride with the captain in charge of the exploration. We've*

now extended the concept to "Cool Science Club,"
an after-school program for K-8 that uses physicists,
teachers, meteorologists, and others who know how to
motivate and challenge kids. High school kids also as-
sist in the program that meets one day a week for four
to six weeks. Again, we use experts such as someone
from MWRA (Massachusetts Water Resources Author-
ity) who teaches "Water Water Everywhere."

Lanie is a big proponent of using community resources who enrich the curriculum. Retired scientists come into Lanie's classroom with demonstrations and experiments to share their love of science, to help the children understand that science is relevant to the world today, and perhaps to inspire these youngsters to pursue someday a fascinating career in scientific work. She coordinates activities with RE-SEED (Retirees Enhancing Science Education through Experiments and Demonstrations), a Northeastern University community outreach program. Lanie provides experiential learning opportunities by taking her students on valuable field trips to explore Boston Harbor, the Museum of Science, and the New England Aquarium. She has even had them involved in testing the pH and overall water quality in the river that runs through the town center.

There's a huge reservoir of talent in the community! I
welcome people to share their expertise, money, and
materials; and they in turn like to participate with
kids. They love our kids' energy and responsiveness
and see them as our hope, our future. I think it's really
important to talk to our volunteers ahead of time, giv-
ing them the context of what we're doing, the vocabu-
lary, reviewing their activities, and making sure that
their presentations are not just lecture or power point
presentations. Otherwise, kids will glaze over. We talk
about giving kids a hook for learning and how to trig-

ger ideas so students will be engaged. From experience, I've learned that the visit is best when teachers stay in the room and assist. The whole exchange takes time but its results are multifaceted for kids. Our students get to learn lots more about science; they get a taste of what a particular career is like; and they are connecting with people in the community. The same is true when working with parents. You never know when someone has expertise. When working with fruit flies and asking the parents to help at home with making traps, two valuable people came forward: a researcher involved with thoracic research using fruit flies and another scholar at Harvard. They were great!

Lanie has written and received nine grants for her school, for creating a butterfly garden to researching learning styles and "Bringing the Ocean Indoors." She is a colleague in the true sense of the word, sharing her passion for teaching through formal workshops on current strategies and methodologies as well as in informal discussions of best practices. One would think that it would be enough for one person to be an extraordinary teacher, but not so for Lanie. She is the Curriculum Director for the Middle School Science Department, an active member of the Professional Development Committee, and an invaluable member of the district's Science Program Review Team. As co-advisor to the McCall Community Service Club, Lanie juggles such projects as knitting for shelters, organizing the collection of eight hundred "Toys for Tots," cleaning up the environment in school and in town, and singing for elders. In response to the need for Hurricane Katrina victims, she organized a community-wide whiffleball tournament, which raised thousands of dollars and created great community spirit. Knowing the importance of "community" both in and out of the school, this "doer" is a positive role model for her students. Lanie's intelligence, creativity, caring, and boundless energy make her a superb colleague, and good citizen.

Lanie was asked to speak to new teachers on opening day of school. She offered words of wisdom based on her years of experience— S.M.I.L.E.

"S" is for Smile: When kids enter the classroom, I think of them as if they're actually coming into my home. "I'm so glad that you're here. How was your weekend?" Some students never have people smiling at them. They're not sure of themselves. I want to make sure that I welcome them in the learning environment.

"M" is for Motivate: How can I hook kids into learning? I make it real for them. Everything I do I try to connect with the real world. Here are some examples when I approach a new theme. "We've been hired for the project. You are engineers for Toys R Us. You will develop designs for the best paper airplanes, which consumers will buy." I get materials that they will test, and embrace them flying their planes around the room. When teaching "matter," I might begin, "The Rovers on Mars have sent us information that we have to classify." We'll look at all the properties, liquid for example, to establish density, to see if it can freeze, and to determine what else might be there on the planet. All the learning has to have a purpose, and kids are really successful when it's relevant.

"I" is for It's All About Them! I've learned that it's not about me anymore. It's about them. Once students walk into my classroom, I'm in touch with them and their needs of the moment. Do they need pencils? If so, I give it to them. I don't waste time thinking about or dealing with the issue of not being prepared. I look at the kids. If one looks like he's having a really bad day, I go over and quietly, check in, and offer comfort.

"L" is for Lifelong Learning. It's important to know from the get-go that it's necessary to take courses and keep up with the latest trends. I share my own leaning experiences with my students so they understand that even I am serious and committed to learning more. Mentoring can take many forms for the new or veteran teacher. Have a teacher that you trust to come and observe you. She can pinpoint what's wrong if you're having a problem. Maybe the kids aren't paying attention. She can make suggestions that perhaps the seating arrangement needs tweaking; you're standing in one place and could move around the room more; you're spending more time looking at the right side of the room than the left.

"E" is for Enthusiasm. You must be enthusiastic! It's contagious, like being at a Red Sox game. When planning purposeful lessons, I think what my students would like to do. I make sure all curricula meet the state frameworks; it fits into real life. We reflect on what we've learned, and there are constant assessments such as short quizzes, checking of lab journals, notes and activities.

To teach is to love...your content area, your kids. After all these years, I feel that even more so. In science, my goals are for kids to understand the world around them and to give them the tools to be able to do that. One of my fondest memories is of the last day of school when I saw a kid opening a door, and exclaiming, "Hello World!" He was ready to go into that world and explore it, with his expression saying, "I understand you, and I can take you on!"

Matt Torrens, 2007

He makes high school history vivid and real through simulations, group projects, stimulating lectures, and historical field trips.

Their eyes open wider, and the lights in them grown brighter as they expand their views of the universe. Students in Matt Torrens' Social Studies class at Saratoga High School in the Los Gatos-Saratoga Union High School District in California experience the joy of discovery by delving into history and connecting it with the present. Matt makes history come alive for students. His enthusiasm is contagious, as evidenced by his students' academic performances and their participation in extracurricular activities, including history forays during vacations, an after-school History Club, and volunteer efforts at the local historical society.

Matt's classroom simulations stimulate students in their development of higher-level critical thinking skills while creating lasting memories of content and context.

> *I've always thought simulations are a good way to actively involve kids, which helps their memories, too. Early on, I purchased prepared simulations, but found that I was always adding components to them to make them more interesting for kids. The most successful ones I've used are those I've developed. The one that students remember most came about when I was at home having a "sock war" with my kids. What better way to teach about World War I! Briefly, the rules are laid out as we make two lines of desks to form trenches. If a student is hit with a sock, he has to stand aside for twenty seconds, which leads to a reading and discussion about trench warfare. Next, we have a "tank battle" with blankets over the desks with kids trying to break through, and we discuss the new*

weaponry like machine guns. Then two pilots, wearing swim goggles, grab as many socks as they can carry and get to walk in the trench undeterred, which leads us to learn about the new airplane technology that was developed. Finally, students bring their "stinky socks" for another dogfight, when we learn about gas being used in warfare. Throughout the lessons, we discuss the various effects of war on people, the industries involved in building destructive machines, and the difficulties of getting through barriers. I enhance the readings and simulations with film excerpts from PBS' "Great War" so students can see images. They view women in factories, which leads to further talk about women's rights (They could participate in war but they couldn't choose their leaders.), the suffragette movement, and the political effects.

During the year, we'll have trials, a Constitutional Convention where delegates from each state are assigned to address the issues of representation, whether to scrap the Articles of Confederation, and slavery, and many other simulations. As a teacher, I really have to balance breadth vs. depth. I have to ask myself, "Will they remember a lecture, or will they remember a simulation?" I've found that if I can supplement a simulation with readings and meaningful activities like a movie, guest speaker, or review of a primary document, I'll go with the simulation. By using several challenges to recreate the events or issues and getting the students to actively participate, I have a better shot at getting history to stick with my students.

Matt's students and their parents appreciate his efforts. His colleagues comment, "Watching him lecture is similar to watching a performer. His eyes light up as he dramatically tells historical stories with the intrigue and detail found in *People* magazine. He emphasizes the tidbits of historical figures' lives, which captivates his students." His students say they enjoy his class because "Mr. Torrens is excited about history." They like the way he relates the subject to sports, current movies, and other areas of typical teenagers' lives. He might compare the Civil War to the movie *The Matrix,* or have students dress in 1960s apparel while discussing that turbulent period.

> *I get so caught up in the activities that I'm enjoying them myself. This is critical. Make the lesson fun and participatory, and students will enjoy the material. Enthusiasm overrides a lot of inadequacy. Kids will remember the smile, the raising of tone, the drama; and they will want to be a part of it!*

"Local History is Sexy!" is a sign on Matt's classroom wall. Matt believes that kids need to connect with their community, and he makes this happen through historical field trips and local working tours in Los Gatos and Saratoga, accompanied by a lot of storytelling.

> *I live in a community similar to many in this area where there is a lot of immigration, and there tends to be little connection to the tradition and heritage of the community. So my goal is to get my students interested in local history and see their community as more than a shopping center or grocery store. One of their assignments is to contribute two hours at the Saratoga Museum of Local History, where they might transcribe the oldest diary of the town, create displays, or comb through boxes of newspapers and file them in categories, and then digitize them. Often my classes do hands-on projects that support the town. One year I worked with a group of interested students and the city of Saratoga to establish a World War II Memorial. On the last day*

of the year, we take a two-hour tour of Saratoga where we visit the cemetery, specific houses, and memorials. We look at the architecture, talk about personalities, and discuss political and social history, like the prohibitionist who lived in the town. John Brown's wife is buried here in Saratoga, and this very high school has three Academy Award winners. Kids are fascinated. It's been worth the effort of researching the material and putting it all together.

During December vacation, I meet about fifty kids at the train station for our annual "Manifest Destiny" field trip to San Francisco. We start in Chinatown, the setting for lots of events taking place during the California Gold Rush and the Mexican American War. We ride the cable car, with some kids racing uphill on foot to see who gets to the top first. Then we explore Nob Hill, an affluent district that is home to many of the city's old money families, and the old Fairmount Hotel, which has a view of the whole bay. We end up in Union Square, which was named on the eve of the Civil War as demonstration of support for the Union.

We take bigger field trips, too, like our experience through parts of Utah and Colorado to learn about the Wild West. We took a trip to Washington D.C. to be part of President Obama's inauguration, with side trips to museums and Civil War battlefields. Kids learn a lot!

Matt believes in pushing every kid to his or her limits, enough so to "make each one a little uncomfortable." He makes sure to provide differentiated instruction that allows different types of responses to an assignment or activity.

It takes time to create instruction and assessment that are varied, yet I think it's important to create different activities to meet the different needs and interests of my students. Even within a high performing A.P. History class, there are kids who have a range of talents and need to have opportunities that are challenging but are equitable with regard to different levels of performance. I make sure that activities and essential questions are broad enough so my students can complete them and be successful. There's always encouragement to do more. For advanced students, I add, "If you have a further question about the material, answer it. I'm eager to see more information or additional quotes that you can find to support your thesis." Typically, the students rise to my high standards.

The National History Project provides another example of differentiated instruction. It is a national competition that is research-based and offers an individual or small group (Most kids tend to work in small groups.) choices of a broad-based project such as a ten page paper, web site, or documentary. We don't have time to incorporate this activity during class time, so it's held after school. The project is a good fit for the History Club, which I coordinate. We brainstorm possibilities for the theme. This year it was "Individuals in History: Legacies and Actions," and fifteen to twenty kids focused on figures such as Bono, Einstein, and Frank Lloyd Wright. I think this is a great activity. Kids have to be independent; they do it by choice, and they get a great sense of accomplishment. They make presentations to the History Department, adults at the county and state levels, and their classmates. The projects are also displayed in the lobby. One of our councilmen was so impressed by the projects that he supported the idea of sponsoring an annual student scholarship upon graduation.

Matt reflects on his many teaching experiences, and his very first one offers insights for new and veteran teachers.

I taught in a ghetto of Washington D.C., which was surrounded by projects. I was one of three teachers in a school of three thousand students. It was there that I learned that kids need to be kids, and teachers need to be responsive even if it means stopping a lesson. "M," a student, came eighty percent of the time and often waited for me to open the door. This time he walked to the window, looked outside at the ghetto, and told me the story of a friend who was shot and killed during the past week. We talked a bit. He was distant and not involved. I still ask myself, "Should I have stayed more with him?" because I never saw him again. It was the time of the Million Man March in Washington, when many were saying, "Build yourself up from your own bootstraps." I learned that the next time I noticed a kid in distress, I would put my lesson plan on hold and reach out to him. I was too focused on what had to be done—the next activity and the next assignment. It was easier to get caught up in the four walls around me. So, years later, I take time every Monday morning for the first ten minutes to talk with kids about what their lives are like. This makes me more empathetic and helps me to step into their world. They see that I care and I'm interested in them. This weekly chat gives me something to further talk about when I see kids in the hallway, lunchroom, or ball field. We can discuss the dance, the driver's license, the game. As teachers, we need to get out of our classroom configuration and really connect with kids in a different way.

In addition to his regular teaching responsibilities, Matt has been an athletic coach, has served as the school's Site Council chairperson for three years, and is the advisor to the Model United Nations Club, the Cricket Club, and the History Club. He also serves as the Santa Clara County Coordinator for the National History Day competition, consults for the District's Peer Assistance and Review Program (PAR), and acts as a site supervisor for a new teacher through National University. It is no surprise that Matt was voted as the Teacher of the Year for the Los Gatos-Saratoga Joint Union High School District for 2006. He is an outstanding teacher, mentor, and leader in his school community.

> *From fourth grade on, I've never wanted to be anything but a teacher. I had a talent for standing up in front of others and talking. I'm fortunate to have had different teaching experiences in Utah, Washington D.C., Japan, and Saratoga; and I always had good role models. I love to study and teach history!*

෨෨

Igniters: To Worlds Beyond

The protagonist in *The Shadow of the Wind,* a novel by Carlos Ruiz Zafon, reveals his first thought upon waking, "I have to tell my friend about the Cemetery of Forgotten Books," a secondhand bookstore where he planned to explore books written by a particular novelist. "I pictured us both, equipped with flashlights and compasses, uncovering the mysteries of those bibliographic catacombs" (11). Another friend, a blind woman whose "vision" is set aflame by books, shares her delight for books. "Never had I felt trapped, seduced, and caught up in a story, the way I did with that book. Until then, reading was just a duty, a sort of fine one had to pay teachers and tutors without knowing why. I had never known the pleasure of reading, of exploring the recesses of the soul, of letting myself be carried away by imagination, beauty, and the mystery of fiction and language. For me all those things were born with that novel" (27).

Lightning bolts that ignite students come in different forms that fire students for further discovery: special interest books suggested by a knowledgeable librarian, hands-on experiments provided by classroom teachers that lead to new revelations, field trips that spark curiosity, and shared experiences of a social action project. Educators have a mission to ignite sparks of light. They speak of their joy when beholding the "ahas" of understanding in their students' eyes. They live for those moments when their charges make mental connections in solving problems, transfer knowledge, and generate creativity. And they don't leave important "habits of mind," including purposeful-learning, critical and creative thinking, and multiple enrichment opportunities, to chance. These skills are incorporated with content over time so students have many instances to practice them. Never passive about the practice of teaching, educators reflect, question, modify, and add to their repertoire of methods and materials to engage children in active, joyful learning. They ask themselves the question, "Should all students be involved in learning the same content, or might it be different for those with different talents, interest, and aspirations?" They recognize that for the full spectrum of learners, there is a need to differentiate curriculum, respecting the needs, interests, and talents of their students.

One of their core beliefs is maximizing resources, their own and those of others in the broader community. They seize the moments and the opportunities to share the passions, talents, interests, and experiences of those eager to expand the minds of children at all levels from kindergarten to high school. Educators recognized for excellence by the Goldin Foundation are known for their willingness to continue learning throughout their professional lives, their passion for working with children, and their desire to create numerous opportunities for enrichment. The following "snapshots" offer some insights about how they provide enrichment.

Aja Mahoney, 1995 *Family and community enjoy learning together.*
A kindergarten teacher from Needham, Massachusetts, Aja brought her own farm experiences into her classroom with a multitude of cooking and craft projects that integrated all subject areas. Each year she held a kindergarten picnic on her Trelawney Farm in Freemont, New Hampshire. The picnic included horse and pony rides, frog catching in the duck pond, fishing, nature walks, and a variety of other activities that are only available on a working farm. About one hundred fifty students and their families took part on these special days.

Susan Logsdon, 1991 *Interdisciplinary learning on the world stage occurs in first grade.*
A first grade teacher in Dover-Sherborn, Massachusetts, Susan was recognized for creating major thematic units that integrated diverse curriculum areas with related skills for an extended

period, possible even for first graders who are thought to have limited attention spans! Goals of the unit on Japan, for example, were to compare and contrast the U.S.'s culture and Japan's, to perceive and value differences, to create global awareness while strengthening children's skills and talents, and to give every child an opportunity for success. All of the classroom strategies and activities reflected these goals within disciplines of art, literature, language, writing, drama, music, geography, social studies, physical education, cooking, science, and math.

Mariana Alwell, 2006 *Academics plus exciting hands-on activities increase understanding.*

Mariana, a fourth-fifth grade teacher at the Garden Gate School in Cupertino, California, makes learning come alive. To understand a math concept or historical event better, she and her students frequently wear costumes, dance, role-play, or use manipulatives. Her students, for example, become experts on one aspect of ancient Egypt and then act as docents for the rest of the school during the two-day Garden Gate Egyptian Museum, which Mariana originates. In all situations, students are expected to be active learners, building their own understandings through discussion, hands-on activities, and in-depth research. They are challenged to be flexible in their thinking when looking for other methods to solve a problem or trying to see another point of view.

Holly Arthur, 2002 *Physical education combines with real-world applications.*

A physical education and health teacher at the Cunniff Elementary School in Watertown, Massachusetts, Holly integrates academic content and physical education activities. Through a grant that she wrote, Holly acquired heart monitors for students in her classes, which were used to learn about the correlation between exercise, fitness, and one's heart. For Black History

Month, Holly designed balance and coordination exercise activities by devising an obstacle course for students to navigate. These activities were linked to the Underground Railroad by the use of labels and later discussions focusing on difficulties navigating the terrain.

Lynn Moore Benson, 1997 *Foreign language and technology accelerate learning.*

Lynn, a French teacher at the Wellesley Middle School in Massachusetts, was into applications of technology that were trend setting, long before they were utilized in most school settings. Her students watched and listened to videos of native speakers, recorded specific phrases from the videos, and received immediate feedback by allowing them to hear their pronunciation followed by the native pronunciation of the same expression. Students became quite comfortable using other creative applications of technology such as the Internet to gather information about French-speaking countries. They even dialogued with students in some of these countries. Lynn utilized video for years as a method for having students gain a better understanding of the French language. Students used Hyperstudio software and Aldus Persuasion software to incorporate maps and other visual materials into their reports and create slide shows, which illustrated their knowledge. Of particular note was Lynn's involvement in the only national school pilot for video editing software. All of these programs accelerated the rate at which her students learned listening and speaking skills.

Leslie Codianne, 1991 *Critical thinking and problem solving take place in special education.*

A special education teacher at Holliston Middle School in Massachusetts, Leslie was recognized for her leadership in the design and implementation of programs that mainstreamed all special education children into regular classes. Co-authoring a science project called "Discovery: Sail and Survival," Leslie developed a hands-on curriculum that included units on navigation, sailing, orienteering skills, and the actual building of model sailboats. The goals of the program were to develop navigational and survival skills taught in the "Voyage of the Mimi," providing students with opportunities for problem solving and independent thinking. The focus was also on social interaction, with many opportunities for students to test their hypotheses. Leslie often came back to school in the evening to help the students and parent volunteers construct their models. Each week after school, she also took students sailing on a nearby lake. The project developed collaboration among the school, parents, and business community.

Gary Stockbridge, 2007 *World history and world literature combine for meaningful learning.*

Gary, a social studies teacher at Medfield High School in Massachusetts, leaves a positive imprint on all the people he meets. He taught honors sophomore students in a combined humanities program of world history and world literature he pioneered twenty-five years ago, "Modern World Conflicts." Gary led his students to think critically about historical events and periods and to consider their own responsibilities as members of our global society. Each student's culminating six-month project from the humanities course was a forty-five minute film or videotaped play that explored a major theme in world history and literature throughout different historical periods. These projects were often used when students applied to colleges. Students worked hard, produced exceptional work, and learned life lessons all along the way.

Michael Alan, 2006 *The town embraces an annual student film festival.*

Michael is an English teacher and advisor to the Walpole High School Film Festival and *The Cricket Literary Magazine*, in Walpole, Massachusetts. He is best known around town for instituting a film festival, which involves not only students but also faculty, administration, and the entire Walpole community. It has become one of the town's favorite events. Students in the "Screenwriting" class write scripts; and production crews storyboard, video, and edit using iMovie and Final Cut software. A recent "Spring Film Festival" had eight movies plus one international film, which was shot in Spanish and shown with English subtitles. Mike does the whole "Oscar" scene, arranging for filmmakers to be delivered by limos, a red carpet for the arrivals, and a student shot documentary of the festival. A panel of faculty and student judges votes on awards for best screenplay, student actors, faculty actors, director, and cinematographer.

Each day brings its unexpected surprises. Each year brings its own class with its own personality. What is consistent about these educators of excellence is their flexibility, sense of humor, and risk taking. They are always involved in trying new ideas and strategies to keep education fresh and exciting. That means reinventing themselves at times, perhaps taking on the challenge of a new grade level or role. They seek to improve themselves personally and professionally as they strive to come up with new strategies to address the needs, interests, and talents of students. They are creative and think out of the box. "Enthusiasm is contagious," they say. "If you're excited, the children will be too." These educators of excellence empower their students to rise to new heights and explore the splendors of worlds beyond.

෧ல

Angela DiNapoli, 1998

A creative elementary teacher, she developed a highly interactive "Astro-Saucer" unit that gets students to explore worlds beyond.

During many of her vacation periods, you will find Angie DiNapoli participating in a space launch or visiting NASA as a teacher scholar to broaden her curriculum. A fifth grade teacher at the Newman Elementary School in Needham, Massachusetts, Angie is a shining star casting bursts of light to her students, who respond in kind. She is an outstanding example of what a teacher must be if the United States is to be tops in science and technology in the twenty-first century.

Angie possesses a contagious enthusiasm for science. Long before it became fashionable, she replaced textbook teaching with real experiments and real "things" that demand that students manipulate both their hands and their brains.

> *Throughout my life, science has been a love of mine. While some teachers question, "How can I integrate science into other curriculum areas," I have always asked, "How can I integrate other curriculum areas into my science units?" From my experiences with children, I have discovered that they are naturally motivated and curious about science, and so it is the perfect "hook" for engaging children in the learning process.*

Angie's best-known work is a space simulation program, "The Astro Saucer," which has been institutionalized in Needham with all fifth graders participating in the units and lessons she created. The program has students playing the role of "aliens" from an alien planet traveling through our solar system to Earth, its final destination. Angie raised funds to have a cold air inflatable flying saucer that is a futuristic space transportation system, or "flying saucer." It is twenty feet long and has eight to ten interior activity stations. There are three phases to the multidisciplinary curriculum.

- Phase one is the creation of an alien planet, which combines scientific facts and creativity.
- Phase two involves astronaut training experiments, which deal with docking, weightlessness, re-hydrating foods, and communication skills. The pre-mission stage is a cooperative effort to create a crew satellite, patch, message to Earth, experiment, and develop an exercise program. The mission stage takes place in the flying saucer, where children experience eating, sleeping, and working in space. They experiment with fluids in space, the movement of a frictionless car, binary code messages, a disorientation maze, identifying Earth locations from space, and exercising in space.
- The last phase has the children working in cooperative groups as scientists exploring Earth. The zoologists study and classify animals. Botanists study and identify plants around the school. Meteorologists use weather instruments to predict the weather and draw conclusions about heat energy. Archeologists excavate and assemble a human skeleton. Physicists experiment with the properties of light. Finally, the geologists classify and identify rock and mineral samples through a series of investigations.

The entire experience connects all areas of the curriculum—reading, writing, and math—with hands-on and cooperative activities for students. Angie continues to adapt her model with students, colleagues, and parents in order to keep the program fresh and exciting. She has created additional learning stations that review science concepts taught in previous grades—a helpful connection for students who must take MCAS state exams. For example, the plant station now includes a dissection of plants to reinforce learning of its different parts and identifying leaves with trees. In addition, electricity is reviewed by hands-on experiments with circuits.

I've had some incredible learning experiences of my own while developing the space unit. Early in my career, I took NASA workshops, went to Space Camp, and the Space Academy in Colorado. I started communicating with experts in the field so that I could better create meaningful activities for my students. When offered a tour at Johnson Support Center, which was working on life support systems, I jumped at the chance. My superintendent supported me, granting me the time for a "take advantage of the moment" opportunity. While in Houston, I learned that my 6th grade student Sunita Williams (Suni) was applying to be an astronaut. I distinctly remembered her coming to school with a wet head every day, as she was a determined young lady training for a swim team. By luck or fate, I met her while on tour, and we began an eight-year correspondence during her training. My students and I were the fortunate recipients of videos showing her at work in both space and underwater habitats; we exchanged email questions and answers. I was even invited to attend the launch and received VIP treatment.

During her time in space, Suni communicated with our class via the space station via video conferencing and emails. Each week she sent a mystery picture of what was in space and challenged the students to find out what it was and relay the answer. Our class kept up with Suni as she trained for the Boston Marathon in space, learning about her exercise program and the machines used. After her mission, Suni came to Needham and visited our class as well as interacted with students during a whole school assembly. When the town decided to develop a preschool playground based on a space theme, our students devised a grand follow-up to our own space exploration. They decided to write their own picture books for preschoolers that would be laminated and attached to playground benches for younger kids to read. One picture book is an alphabet book. Each page, which is written by a different child, has a real space fact, picture, and alliterative prose. For the letter S: "Sunita soared through the sky into space in STS 116 so she could see the spectacular stars in space." Suni later autographed these and other books that she liked to read as a young child, and little ones in the playground enjoy them.

Angie has always used parents as valuable resources in her class. At the first parents' conference at the beginning of the school year, she polls her parents to learn about their interests and talents. She gives them an overview of the topics she teaches and asks whether they would be interested in coming in to talk, demonstrate, and participate in activities with the students.

It's about making connections, incorporating content, curriculum, and careers. Making time for enrichment that kids wouldn't have is so important, even in these days of heavy focus on testing. I make the time for it. Otherwise, it would be a missed opportunity. Parents and even their relatives and friends become important allies in the learning process. For my unit on "Pioneers," I have people coming back to participate even after fifteen years—former students too. The opportunity to utilize parent resources doesn't have to be limited to the elementary school. I certainly would recommend that the practice be encouraged at the other levels too, for visitors convey their excitement of travel, real life skills, and understandings about their own process of development. Typically, they convey, "If I can do this, you can too!"

Angie served as science curriculum facilitator for Needham, and she is currently developing additional interdisciplinary science units and working on a science committee to align Needham science curriculum with the Massachusetts State Frameworks. She's working with colleagues on another new initiative that has been well received. The "PLC" or Professional Learning Collaborative emphasizes giving teachers at each grade level time during the school day to review and evaluate instruction, discuss the pros and cons before jumping into new programs, and develop and implement pilots. Angie has also taught college level courses at local universities and presented her ideas at regional and national conferences.

There are consistently "new" programs and demands on teachers coming from state and local levels, which often create stress...more testing, for example. I think testing children is important, but it shouldn't be used as an assessment of the teacher. Give teachers tools to teach, ideas and time, for example; and the test scores will improve.

It's good to be innovative, but change takes time. I believe that change should start from the teachers upward and not from the administration downward. The most beneficial experiences come from teachers teaching teachers.

To be a good teacher, one must also be a lifelong learner, and learning is not a solitary venture. Throughout my years as an educator, I have been influenced by many people. My family offers me wonderful support; my principals have encouraged me to try new ideas and methods with my students; and I have been fortunate to have taught with excellent colleagues who have helped me to grow professionally. From them I have learned

interpersonal skills and various techniques for commu-
nicating with parents and students.

Teachers are learners. They can't possibly know
everything. They are constantly learning new content,
new strategies for instruction, classroom management,
communication, and just the everyday "how tos." The
biggest resources are other teachers. Collaboration is
essential. A new teacher needs a mentor, and an experi-
enced teacher can learn from a new teacher. My advice
for a new teacher is: "If the match isn't there, advo-
cate for yourself and find someone who's a better fit."
Collaborating with a teaching partner, I have expanded
my repertoire of teaching strategies. They include cur-
rent techniques in accelerative learning, and coopera-
tive learning. I've applied Howard Gardner's theory of
Multiple Intelligence, brain compatibility, and learning
style theories for working with students in an inclusion
classroom. (I just love having an inclusion class. The
whole atmosphere of learning changes as all children
learn patience and tolerance. Everyone is prized for
something he or she is really good at.) My newest part-
ner is a very young teacher, and together we plan, strat-
egize, and engage in creative thinking. I'm never alone
as I seek connections with my peers. I choose not to be
a person locked in a room for I would be closed down
creatively, and I love the professional camaraderie.

Education is constantly changing. To grow profession-
ally, teachers must also change. But I suggest that we
be selective. It's not always prudent to jump on every
new bandwagon. Some current theories are really pre-
vious educational practices with newer names. Read,
attend workshops and courses, and learn about new

techniques. Be a risk taker and try the ones that are interesting and seem valid. Keep adding to your repertoire. And whenever possible, share your success stories with other colleagues. Encourage growth and learning in other colleagues, as well as your students. My vision for myself is to continue to have fun in my teaching career and to show my students that learning is fun and a lifelong goal.

If I could change something during my long career, I would better balance my professional and personal lives. I would set limits and definitely find a part of every day to do something for myself whether it's picking up a book, working out, or just relaxing.

I'm profoundly fulfilled as a teacher. When I have students contact me long after I've had them in class, I realize how much impact teachers really have on students. They do remember us. We've inspired them, and they have continued to inspire me. I enjoy getting up each day, for what could be more exciting than having a major influence on children one hundred eighty days a year? It's incredible!

∽

Judith Paradis, 2007

This media specialist is "No Ordinary Book Lady." A force of energy, she is teacher, mentor and role model to her whole school community.

Judith Paradis switches on the lights of learning at Plympton Elementary School in Waltham, Massachusetts. She brings smiles to children's faces because they think they're the most special persons in the world when they are around her; she's a valuable resource to teachers; and her colleagues note that she renews vitality to her school community. "She came to us like a breath of spring, so refreshing, so creatively enthusiastic. She immediately energized everyone, child and teacher alike. Very quickly, noticeable changes included unlimited borrowing of books, reading contests, and school-wide projects." Judi takes the time to talk or to listen carefully to each student, thus empowering thoughts and valuing ideas. Her conversations are often punctuated with the words, "How cool is that!" Judi seems to know each and every child and his or her individual interests and always seems to come up with the just the right books. Her enthusiasm about books is contagious with library being a "favorite time," enough so that students often choose to go there during indoor recess to curl up with books.

> *Being a librarian is so different from the image that people have. One great result of the Goldin award was the excitement shared by other librarians that I was recognized for excellence as a teacher. I spend the majority of my time teaching and co-teaching. Teachers often bring their classes to the library for instruction in social studies or science, and I'm there to assist. Every class comes to the library at least once a week, and I first have a group discussion with the kids before they're let loose to find their books. It might be about researching a topic. I take them through the*

process, which I repeatedly do during their six years. "What's the big question? What are the little questions you need to discover? What materials make sense for this project? What kind of books might you need?" I then have time to work individually with students, be it finding a book that is appropriate to their reading levels or checking in with them on finding authentic resources for their research. The classroom teacher is present, which reinforces the research process. Previously we worked together to plan projects in content areas that really grabbed the kids. By the time kids leave our school, they have a comfort level with the library. They know it's a fun place to read or readily get information about fiction and non-fiction subjects; they're competent with technology; and they know that their knowledge is applicable elsewhere in other libraries, schools, and homes.

Judi knows her materials and resources and is well versed in the curriculum at each grade level, as she brainstorms and plans formal lessons with each teacher.

I get a chance to informally meet with teachers when they come with their classes for library period, and I have regular meetings with individual teachers, sometimes at grade meetings. I also keep up-to date with the prescribed curriculum, the MA Framework guides, reading journals and conferences, and teachers' individual interests, such as their travels. Early on I'll send out a memo, "What are the big things coming up this year for which you need support?" I might say, "I see you're doing folktales; here's three cool books and some ideas." "Here's some new books I've found for your unit on American Indians." "This internet

*source might be a good one to tie in with fractions."
"Let's chat about integrating concepts with the school
theme." Teachers have great ideas, which I honor, so I
try to be very supportive, and I've found the teachers to
be very responsive.*

Judi believes that with the ever-accumulating amounts of information
children receive, research skills are even more important to develop.
She supports teacher instruction by helping to coordinate grade-level
research projects. She provides formal class instruction while paying
attention to individual needs, such as photocopying articles and finding reference books that match each child's reading ability. Often she
orchestrates research projects so that each child becomes an "expert"
in a study area and then shares his knowledge with classmates. Adding
to the enrichment of the whole school, she videotapes each child's presentation, so parents unable to attend can borrow the tapes or classes
can review the material.

*Clearly, there is a generation divide in that teachers
don't have the same experience in technology as kids.
This leads to some interesting and unanswered issues
regarding the use of technology for research and classroom work. 1) How can we teach students and teachers
appropriate information literacy as well as information fluency? Where do they start to access information
when there is so much communication and information
with seven hundred plus TV channels, the Internet, pod
casts, and blogs? Perhaps we should focus on how to
make sense of all the information out there and ask
if we are getting the right information from the right
source. For instance, is Wikipedia, which many people
reference, a good source? Perhaps we can view Wikipedia as a first pass before we explore further; we need
to be careful as to what we will or won't accept as the*

final authority. Here's an idea for teachers that worked with students. One study group of students was getting ready for a big project on Asia. They picked an article in Wikipedia and their jobs were to verify every Wiki fact by looking at online journals, databases, published works, websites of public television and universities. Their conclusion—"keep researching!"

2) How much of this new technology leads to more glitz than substance? We assume that kids are smart because of their ability to manipulate technology-leading products that look great. Are we focusing on the content, which inherently is more important? When we are asking for quality work, are we focusing on critical thinking?

3) We are in the middle of a profound shift in knowing how kids think and learn about things. In contrast to how we learned, kids show differences in reaction time, which is faster, and attention span, which is shorter, largely due to the fast pace of TV and new technology. They're so comfortable with technology that they will do things in the future of which we aren't even aware. Even now, there are programs that are tailored to different learning styles. Virtual travel and talking to people in faraway places are common. I'm still concerned about the needs to teach critical thinking skills and to focus on essential questions, those big overarching ideas, while we involve our kids in project-based learning. Technology can serve as valuable tools for accessing this knowledge. For example, one third grade class studying animals and plants was challenged with questions such as: What difficulties might animals and plants have in different climate areas of desert, tundra,

or tropical rainforest; how would they adapt? Students'
tasks were to compile a book and drawings based on
their research. One child even built diagrams of the dif-
ferent land forms on the computer.

Plympton School has a very diverse population and promotes engagement of all children in learning about the various cultures it represents.
Judi, in collaboration with others, established a school-wide program
that focuses on one continent all year. This allows for exposure to in-
depth study of cultures, histories, and geographies of all six continents
during the primary years. A series of activities runs throughout the
year and also involves parents, artists, and the broader community.

It's a chance to explore concepts in depth, acknowl-
edge the wide range of multiethnic populations in each
continent, and empower kids who come from different
countries. Every teacher's challenge is to find ways
of incorporating skills and curriculum areas with the
major theme. For example, with the school-wide study
of Latin America, second graders, who learn about
folktales, compare them with those of Peru and other
countries. Kids who learn about earthquakes, volca-
noes, and tectonic plates map fault lines along the An-
des Mountains. Art, music, and drama are part of the
program, and we do a big production in the spring such
as having kids script a folktale and develop authentic
costumes, scenery, and music. Artists are brought in to
teach Brazilian martial arts and Peruvian music. We
use other special days such as the day before February
vacation when we bring in guests from the community
to share their customs, and Field Day when kids play
games from the cultures studied. There's even a com-
munity service piece where kids take real ownership of
an idea. Last year kids collected $800 for shelters for

the homeless in Guatemala, saved in "house" banks made from milk cartons. The whole process is awesome and so inclusive! Everyone learns so much and there is tremendous community spirit!

There are many other initiatives that Judi has developed and implemented at Plympton.

➤ The *Book Buddy Program* for second and fifth graders meets twice a month and forges relationships over a literature-based activity. The older students read to the younger ones, and they serve as audiences for each other. Judi designs a special activity for each meeting that builds on literacy skills taught in class, and each ends with a final project that is publicly displayed.

➤ To motivate children to read and experience achievement, Judi designs creative reading contests. A very popular one had a baseball theme that required children to work as a team. Other contests are individual. One contest prompted a severely learning-disabled child to compete. This reluctant reader began to devour picture books, had his parent read to him, and listened to books-on-tape. He actually won the contest; if not for Judi's extra efforts, this child wouldn't have had an opportunity to be successful.

➤ Judi raised over $1000 through her Scholastic Books effort. Making sure that no child leaves feeling deprived, Judi coordinates a used book swap during the fall in which all children receive a novel. Everyone, regardless of personal finances, leaves with a book.

➤ Judi secured grants for special programming that impact all students. Some monies were allocated to improve multicultural awareness, such as bringing a group of African dancers and drummers. This resulted in a high level of excitement with children dancing and singing for days.

➤ Judi also runs a weekly enrichment program that targets proficient readers and supports them in student-directed literacy activities, which keeps advanced students motivated, challenged, and excited about learning and reading. It takes considerable time and energy as she prepares for each enrichment class, scaffolds projects, and tracks participant progress.

There is a wide range of learning abilities in grades one and two. It's not until third grade that there is formalized enrichment program for the proficient reader. I meet with each class once a week for thirty-five minutes on a project that is open-ended and on which the children can work after they've completed their classroom assignment. The kids view this as "fun" not "more work." They're challenged with directed activities. I never assume that they know the skills; rather I teach and reinforce study and research skills and habits. First graders might use the Internet to learn more about bats; in literature they might write an end to a story that I've begun; and they develop and present a "Reader's Theater" for the kindergarten. In second grade, kids choose a subject based on interest, from poetry to sports, and use six books for their summary and reflective piece. They have to also explain how each book is different from others in the stack and comment on what they learned. One child was very absorbed in learning about Martin Luther King, and she ended her project by writing a letter to the King Center in Atlanta about what he meant to her.

Kids have been so excited about this library time that when they don't formally have it when they get to third grade, they're upset. So in grades three-six we now have a discussion program during lunchtime about a

book they've read. I even have seventh graders com-
ing back two times a month for their own "club" after
school. I feel that with the emphasis on "No Child Left
Behind" legislation, we sometimes leave the more ad-
vanced behind with less resources for them. They will
be our salvation if we educate them to their potential.

Judi strengthens parental involvement in the library through a volunteer program.

After having my own kids, I have real appreciation for
parents who want to help. It's not an intrusion such as
might be perceived in a classroom. It's a great way for
them to do some very necessary tasks such as checking
and shelving, which frees up my time for instruction.
It's also a nice way to get word out in the community as
to what the library is doing. I'm big on communicating
and will send out emails to the whole group of volun-
teers. "Here's what's going on; here's how you might
be useful; how would you like to help?" And so they
do! On Friday mornings, parents can even bring their
toddlers who "read" in their own section of the library
and have snacks. These kids become library-savvy. We
even have a group of senior citizens who become read-
ing ambassadors to individual students and classes.

Judi offers some insights about her experiences.

If I were to make any changes, I would not have put off
teaching until after my kids were eleven and fourteen. I
would have done this earlier.

I wish that I had had better management skills. I think
a lot can be taught through observation, and I would

recommend this being done more during the mentoring process. I know from co-teaching all day long that I see a lot that I love and some things that I don't, so I adapt what makes sense for me.

If I could offer advice to new teachers, I would encourage them to "stay excited!" Nothing happens without enthusiasm. It's hard not to get caught up in the prescribed material, but that doesn't mean that you can't be creative in application or do some special programming. Reflect on what you really have to do. Read the professional literature; there are so many great ideas. Find a mentor, a person who really wants to help. If the person who's been assigned is not a good match, find one who is.

Some of the best teachers are seen as "subversive," not doing exactly what is prescribed. Yet these are great teachers who are passionate, want to keep fresh, teach about things they love, and try out different ideas each year. We need to inspire those teachers who want to do better. I think we have to do a better job of attracting the best teachers and compensate them appropriately. Then we can have a true renaissance. I'm excited about the new Readiness Project in our state of Massachusetts. There's a range of people involved from college presidents to teachers who are looking at what works and doesn't, and they will make recommendations to the governor. Different communities will read the report and react to it as it meets their individual needs and interests. I am hopeful about the future!

෮

Spotlights: The Whole Child

Nilaja Sun, a brilliant playwright, teacher, and teaching artist, uses her skills as a listener, her own experiences as a learner, and her imagination to enter into the experiences of her students in the hallways and classrooms of urban schools. Her play, No *Child...,* is the true story of her experiences teaching drama to an academically and emotionally challenged class. She takes rude, unmotivated, and undisciplined students, exposes them to performing arts, sets purpose and goals, and gets positive results. In a tour-de-force solo performance, Sun illuminates the stage, using her body, voice, and storytelling skills to create the illusion of a stage full of characters. The students she portrays are involved in planning, designing, and setting priorities for their own education, which Sun considers a "very necessary role in civic life" *(Playbook: Encore. The Performing Arts).* Despite hardships at home, they rise to the expectations of their teacher by completing and writing their personal scripts and acting them. The project culminates with a full production of their play. Sun's play and performance challenge us to consider what we might learn if we were to listen directly to young people as they articulate their experiences and perspectives and give them other forms of expression.

When comparing the present state of music and visual and performing art opportunities in schools to past practices, it is difficult not to recognize that there have been drastic cuts in programs, especially during the past two decades. We used to have instrumental lessons, choruses, and bands at the elementary level, and for some school districts at other levels too. Many districts have had major cutbacks in visual art teachers, while in some schools "art on a cart" is the norm. More and more responsibility for visual and performing arts is ceded to the classroom teacher, who may or may not be inclined to provide instruction and exploration.

Piano teacher Douglas Whynott speaks to the value of music lessons based upon his experiences going into homes and teaching youngsters. He observes, although unproven by major research, that kids who take piano get better grades, and that by providing lessons to their children, parents provide them with something special, an act of caring that brings "all kinds of rewards." His book review of *Note by Note: A Celebration of the Piano Lesson* by Tricia Tunstall in the May 18, 2008 edition of the *Boston Sunday Globe* confirms some of the "rewards awaiting a child who spends years developing technique, discipline, and musical feeling under the tutelage of an accomplished teacher." The author says that for many children, piano lessons constitute the sole relationship they will have with an adult other than their parents (D5). Besides teaching chords and scales, music teachers take students into realms of beauty and feeling they may not otherwise experience. This type of experience could also ring true for children who do not have opportunities for exposure to different expressions of the arts. From households where there is no music played, or pictures on the wall, or books to explore, children still come to their other "home," the school, in which educators can integrate experiences which foster the "whole child."

In a letter to the *Needham Times*, a suburban newspaper in Massachusetts, a high school student, Elizabeth Margolis, as early as March 7, 1991, eloquently pleas for education beyond the three Rs to include: arts, humanities, sciences, physical and health education, foreign language, and history. Margolis writes, "We are the future. We want to be tomorrow's leaders and self-sufficient citizens. And, we need all of these skills by formal instruction and supervised practice in order to develop mentally, morally, and aesthetically" (4).

Educating the whole child implies creating opportunities for each child to shine. There may be footlights and spotlights for some and glorious color, line, and composition for others. All children have the light of expression within them that can be lit from a little glimmer to a full sparkle.

෴

Bill Horewitch, 2006

"You have to reach them before you can teach them," says the "Coach" who uses character education and development in all of his physical education classes.

"Thanks for knowing my name. Thanks for believing in me when everybody else, including me, predicted failure. I don't know what you saw in me. You put up with a lot. Thanks for not giving up. Had to let you know that I'm now in medical school becoming a doctor so I can help people just like you always did." Comments like these from a former fourth grade student, who was in trouble most of the time, reflect the concern and follow-up care of Coach Bill Horewitch, a physical education teacher at Southside Primary School in Cleveland, Texas. The school is in a rural area and serves many children whose families are economically distressed and need the supports and structure of their school. Knowing and teaching 950 students on a K-2 campus each year, Bill has touched many lives in his thirty years in the field of education. All of his contributions center on the social and emotional well being of children, who are taught from an early age to respect one another, take responsibility, care for one another, and make a real difference in other's lives.

Coach Bill turns on the inner lights of his students. With genuine compassion and attention to the whole child: body, mind, and spirit, he focuses on a character development theme in his classes. Bill lets children know that they have choices to make and that each can make a difference with their everyday behavior. He emphasizes the importance of respect, tolerance, citizenship, and character. These character traits are emphasized in class, and they are personified by an "I Make a Difference Wall" in the gym that recognizes children whose good deeds and actions make a difference in the lives of others. Bill also developed the A.C.E. (Attitude, Character, Effort) Program that encourages development of character in all areas of the school.

Very early in my career, I saw a great need for charac-
ter development, and I incorporate that in everything I
do with children. An "I Make a Difference" wall in the
gym does not reward performances in games; rather, it
recognizes those kids who go out of their way to make
a difference in other people's lives through their char-
acter choices. My students work very hard during their
P.E. classes to get their names on this wall. Students
have learned to appreciate and desire the benefits of
socialization, sportsmanship, personal achievement,
and team sports that are achieved through physical ed-
ucation. These benefits will carry them on to a love of
health and make a happier future for our kids.

Bill spends a lot of time talking with children both in and out of class.
"Tell me what you did today in school. Tell me what you learned today that you did not know yesterday. How are your friends doing in
school?" As life lessons for kids in "Making a Difference," Bill encourages by word and deed:

➤ *Importance of cooperation: "If the fingers of your hand quarrel,*
  you cannot pick up a spoon."
➤ *Keep trying: Kids say in unison, "Good, better, best, I'll never*
  take a rest till good gets better and better gets best."
➤ *When words hurt: (Kids take a paper heart, crumble it, and then*
  unfold it.) "Saying sorry may help, but even though you're sorry,
  the creases don't go away. Did you ever leave creases on someone's
  heart or have creases made on yours?"
➤ *You can choose to be a good person, or you can choose to be the*
  person someone says you are: "If someone calls you a name, write
  that word on a piece of paper. For example, write 'dumb,' walk to
  the garbage can, and throw it away forever."
➤ *Keep our community clean: Kids pick up litter to feed the "starving*
  garbage can."
➤ *Encourage and praise others: "We'll listen to positive tattletales."*

Bill is a big believer in family and family involvement with the children. Every year he organizes the "Parent and Family Fitness Day" and the "Parent and Grandparent Day and Activities." Recognizing the need for families to be closer, Coach Bill organizes the "National Family Day" on the school campus. The event, which takes place twice a year, invites parents, grandparents and other caretakers to eat lunch at school with their children and models the importance for families to eat meals together and discuss the day's events. Bill also makes himself available to parents for discussions about individual problems concerning their children. One parent notes, "Thanks to Coach Horewitch, I didn't lose my son to bad influences. He was here when my son and I needed him the most, and I know that he will continue to be an excellent role model for my son as well as my ally to help him when I need it. He is an excellent teacher who includes dignity and respect for everyone."

> *As an educator, I have seen the shift in the nuclear family structure: single parent families, grandparents as primary caregivers, and even in the traditional two-parent households with both parents working outside the home. In the majority of cases, these groups of individuals are overworked, over-extended in outside commitments, and just too stressed to be actively involved with their children's education. Children need and must experience supportive, involved, caring people who communicate to them that someone does care about what they do with their lives on a daily basis. We, as teachers, can create a place where those experiences can be introduced and/or reinforced in a child's life.*

> *I send parents and guardians information about my program at the beginning of each year. We talk about expectations and the importance of reaching out to one's child. We discuss life issues and attempt to reach the*

conclusion that one can change what one can change;
otherwise, we have to change the attitude.

Wanting to have a larger impact on children's lives, especially those who were falling behind in academic areas, Bill developed and began T.O.U.C.H (Teachers Open to Uplifting Children's Hearts). The goal of the program is to make a connection between caring adults and students in need of some special attention. It is designed to let selected students know that there is a person on campus who is always there for them, cares about their feelings and needs, and is willing to help the child feel more positive about himself or herself. Any staff member can volunteer to help. A mentor may sometimes eat lunch with a student or may leave small surprises or notes of encouragement on the student's desk just to let him know there is someone else out there with his best interest at heart. Children experience feelings of worth because of who they are, not because of what they do or do not do. Results have been amazing since T.O.U.C.H. was implemented. Children who were chronic absentees started attending school regularly. Small and big issues that prevented students from learning became issues worked out with a special friend, and more academic success became evident. Children who were discipline problems due to bottled up feelings and issues started showing signs of positive self-esteem. One troubled youngster in second grade wrote, "For the first time someone cares about me and listens. Coach, you have changed my life." Bill is such an exemplary role model that parents request his services as a mentor, and presently he is working with five students.

I noticed that one kid was not playing during many recesses. "Let's throw the ball," I suggested to which he responded, "Why?" He was a hard kid to like. Nonetheless, we threw the ball to each other. Another time, I told him, "I have stuff to set up and I need help." Over time, he became my helper and we did a lot of incidental talking, as he wanted to please me. He could only handle gradual praise. He became one of my T.O.U.C.H. students.

Success is an every day event in gym classes and on Field Days. Children enjoy both events without the stress of competing. The concept has changed from competition, where only gifted athletes succeed, to days where all children participate in a series of fun-filled events; and all children are and feel successful. From the banners and cheers to the final whistles, students love the pure joy of participating. There are no losing teams for students in the field or in the gym. In all situations, children not only play games and participate in physical activities; they also learn problem solving skills, social guidelines, and how to make and become good friends.

> *I am a physical educator who doesn't keep score when games are played. The children know that if they try their best, they are all winners, regardless of the score. Only when children feel good about who they are, about themselves, can they become productive successful citizens. Typically, a child's words become "I did better this time, Coach" instead of "He always beats me." A child's worth is not connected with the performance of another child. This total effort is the most unique aspect of my programs. When a child knows he is accepted because of who he is, then my teaching motto, "Do the right thing because it's the right thing to do, knowing that you can do the other but you don't," is put into action. Character is when no one is looking and there is no reward, which closes the door to the belief that winning is everything, that approval of others is worth everything, and that who I am is determined by how well I do things.*

Coach Horewitch brought the Presidential Physical Fitness Testing Program to Southside, and each spring and fall, first and second graders rise to the challenge with students scoring above national norms in all areas. Some students even achieve the highest honor and receive the Presidential Fitness Award. Bill is always there to honor the students and encourage the others with words and actions letting them know they can do the same. Kindergarten students are invited to the awards ceremony so they can prepare themselves for the coming year's challenges. Sports Camp is another opportunity offered by Bill to his students. For one week during the summer and one week during Christmas break, every child has the opportunity to attend. There is a fee, which is waived if a parent cannot afford the program.

Bill's awards and achievements are numerous. In addition to the 2005–2006 Region 4 Education Service Center Teacher of the Year Award, Bill was a Disney Teacher of the Year nominee. He was recently chosen as a Houston Texans NFL Hometown Hero at a Houston Texans Football Game. Coach Bill's career began in Illinois where he graduated from North Park College, and later he taught in the Chicago area for several years. He received his Masters degree from Prairie View A&M University and has taught in Texas school districts for eighteen years.

> *Father Flanagan of Boy's Town once said, "No man stands as tall as when he kneels down to help a child." Teaching is a process of kneeling down to help a child. All children can learn. We as educators must find the keys to unlock this special vault of a "desire to learn" in each child regardless of what it takes. Teaching is so much more that just imparting knowledge in the subject in which we are trained. Teachers must also look for the positive in each and every child.*

Ever the philosopher/teacher, Bill spins sound advice to new teachers.

> ➢ *Greet each and every class and student with "I'm happy to see you today. I'm so glad you're here." We need to be life teachers and let our kids know "I'm here and I care."*
>
> ➢ *As you journey down the path of teaching, remember that good teachers perform miscellaneous acts of kindness everyday without a second thought. Therefore, in the eyes of a child, the smallest gesture may be heroic indeed. Children spell "love" T.I.M.E.*
>
> ➢ *Just ask, "Is it possible?"*
>
> ➢ *Maintain a sense of humor, and try not to get upset when "all around you" is falling apart. Have a TGIM instead of a TGIF (think Monday).*
>
> ➢ *Call parents when things go right.*
>
> ➢ *Guide students with questions, not answers.*
>
> ➢ *Define your acts by love; spin these acts to hope, and with hope, give children a reason to celebrate. We cannot change the world as it is today, but we can make a difference in the lives of children, one child at a time. You can't change what has happened, but you can change what happens next.*
>
> ➢ *At the end of the day, it's more than the score or the grade on the exam that your students will remember. They pick up immediately on the kind of person you are and how you act towards people.*

Coach Bill's actions, more so that the many awards he has received, reminds those of us in education of what he clearly articulates: *We teach to inspire. We teach to touch a life. We teach to make a difference. We teach to encourage children to believe in themselves, all the while obtaining the necessary education needed to be in a position themselves to make a difference in another's life, in society.*

He reminds us of the "Teacher's Creed:"

I am a teacher.
I can teach:
Anybody
Anything
Anytime.

Even at my worst,
I should be able to teach:
Somebody
Something,
Sometime.

The challenge for me
Is to teach:
Everybody
Everything
Everytime.

I am a teacher.
I can make a difference!

෨

Ginny Croft, 2005

Her instrumental music classes have ripple effects that transfer responsibility, ownership, and discipline to other classes.

Children bask in the sunshine created by Ginny Croft, Band Director at Lovett Elementary School in Houston, Texas. Excited about passing on her expansive view of music to the next generation, Ginny commits herself to both the personal and musical growth of children. She goes above and beyond by following the musical and academic achievements of former students and connecting with them long after they have left elementary school. Her unending efforts are recognized and appreciated by the hundreds of lives she has touched and changed.

Ginny shares her philosophy of teaching:

> *A truly effective teacher approaches her class as a living work of art. One can't paint the picture until one builds the frame. In other words, the first priority in the class-room is to establish and be consistent about reinforcing classroom expectations, rules, and procedures. As these are habituated, the focus turns to the content to be mastered. Therefore, organizational skills are a must for effective teaching.*
>
> *Second, the "painter' (teacher) must be extremely sensitive to the colors chosen for the picture, the atmosphere within the classroom, which is created by both the personal feelings carried into the room by the students and by the teacher's mood of the day. The teacher/painter lightens or darkens a child's day by manipulating this atmosphere, and every effective teacher possesses a palate of techniques to brighten the learning environment in order to intensify the students' involvement in the learning situation.*

Third, every good teacher/painter views his or her handiwork, the mastered learning, with the pride of accomplishment and the humility to acknowledge the efforts of others, fellow teachers and participating students, in the collaborative learning process, thereby enhancing the positive self-esteem of all who contributed to the success. This ensures that the next painting attempt, the next learning task to be mastered, will be taken with added enthusiasm.

My students understand the messages of the music they are mastering, which brightens the learning experience greatly. The result, the finished (musical) paintings are shared with pride for appreciative and often amazed audiences. Throughout the whole process, I encourage my students to do well in all of their classes. I stress the interrelationship of all learning, and motivate them by praising their efforts constantly with the reminder that they must pass all subjects and maintain good conduct in order to perform, to be one of the bright colors in our painting, as we all contribute to the creation and maintenance of a positive school climate. There is a natural ripple effect as the sense of ownership; responsibility and hard work are carried over into students' class work and homework.

Ginny initiated the current Lovett Concert Band Program twenty-nine years ago as a volunteer mother. She displays tremendous organization and patience with a large and diverse student population. Taking young children from all backgrounds, and in a short time, she forms several very cohesive groups of performers.

Individualized instruction within an ensemble setting best characterizes the Lovett Elementary Band program in which children in grades one through five attain remarkable levels of musicianship. First graders utilize the flutophone and second graders the recorder, which prepares them for a rigorous curriculum of music reading for Concert Band membership beginning in third grade. The Concert Band has students in grades three through five, who enter to find the seating chart posted on the wall, the list of numbers to be rehearsed on the chalkboard, and the warm-up scale to be played. They understand the messages of the music they are mastering, which brightens the learning experience. Ginny provides the context. Students have fought the Battle of Borodino from Tchaikovsky's "1812 Overture," lumbered along with elephants in Ippolotov-Ivanoff's "Procession of the Sardar," walked gingerly atop imaginary fences in Edmondson's "Jazz Cat," and grieved with Beethoven upon his deepening deafness in the "Pathetique Sonata."

The Concert Band has received many awards and accolades. The only elementary music program in the state of Texas featured on the Texas Education Agency video, "Assessment in the Arts," the Concert Band has been chosen twice to perform in Walt Disney World's "Magic Music Days," and in 2000 won the opportunity to represent Texas in Washington, D.C.'s Bicentennial "National Festival of the States." The band has also presented clinics three times for the music teachers of Texas at Texas Music Educator's Association's annual conventions in San Antonio, the only Houston School District Band to have been so honored. For the past fifteen consecutive years, it holds trophies for top ratings from all judges, Houston and statewide.

Ginny and her music students build connections with the local community. The interaction is a "win-win" for all. The general public quickly becomes aware of a highly positive example of young people in action, who are excited about sharing their talents and the joy of music. The students are exposed to many different resources within Houston, and they take pride as involved citizens in the community. Student groups present annual concerts for events such as Meyerland community's "Afternoon in the Park," the Westbury Community Fair, the Zoo, and Houston's Museum of Fine Arts. Individual students are also encouraged to perform; and Ginny has prepared them for special community events such as "Little Miss Fiestas Patrias," various Black History Month celebrations, and scouts, church, and civic groups. Each child views him or herself as a valuable musical resource and is rewarded for these voluntary service opportunities with a patch for one's uniform that reads "Lovett Elementary Volunteer Musician."

I have been privileged to lead thousands of elementary and secondary choral and instrumental students into enthusiastic participation in the wonderful, soul-satisfying medium of fine music. Many continue their music studies through high school and college; seven have been Texas All-State winners; and several more have been alternates. The greatest compliment I receive is the frequent statement from "band parents" that the band experience is making a significant difference in their children's lives—that their lives are becoming more focused, more meaningful, and more exciting—and that the school day is becoming a more joyous experience with the success mode spilling over onto their other academic subjects. The latter fact does not surprise me. The famous educator, B.F. Skinner, discovered long ago that "in the presence of joy, people learn three to four times more rapidly."

Peripherally, the knowledge gained from working comprehensively with students of all ages has helped me to assist effectively in teaching my congenitally profoundly deaf, rubella-syndrome daughter to learn to listen well. We used a program in which parents in Canada and the U.S. were given strategies to teach their own hearing-impaired children. My daughter, who has a

Bachelor's of Administration degree from Baylor University, now works in healthcare in CA and speaks over the telephone to the family each Sunday afternoon.

Ginny has written educational materials for, and spoken before, groups of parents and teachers of hearing impaired children. She also published sacred choral music with Emerson Music in California and string orchestra music to excite young string players with Carl Fischer in New York, an activity close to her heart, since she is primarily a violinist.

Ginny's students learn respect, patience, and a sense of accountability, which are applied to their community and world. She takes her profession very seriously and sees herself involved in the larger role of evolving the minds of the future through music education, hard work, and practice. Her skills for demystifying complex concepts and explaining musical concepts using interesting and identifiable examples make a big difference to her students.

To new and veteran teachers, she comments, *I "reinvent the wheel," as it were, every year, discarding techniques and procedures, which have proven to be tangential, so I can make better use of the minutes allotted to me to interact with my learners."*

To others, she reiterates the need for developing the whole person.

The realization that experience in the arts is vital to the creation of a well-adjusted young person is just now dawning upon the scene. Of what use is the ability to make a prosperous living if you don't know how to live? We are at a crossroads. Either we become a society of restless technocrats who do not possess the skills for human communication, or we become a society of enriched lives, enjoying the benefits of humanity at its highest form. The three Rs are far too narrow a curriculum for today's world, and the school systems that educate the total person will produce far better citizens for this planet.

∾

Ruth Mathewson, 2007

She uses performing arts to reinforce academic concepts and delight the broader community.

Excitement, electricity, and enthusiasm are what you feel when you speak to Ruth Mathewson about her teaching. A performing arts teacher at Baker Elementary School in the Moreland School District in San Jose, California, Ruth tells you how blessed she is to be working with children to help them learn through music, dance, and drama. Having taught performing arts for thirty years, her face glows as she relates story after story how performing arts influence children and add to the school and wider community.

> *I try to make everything joyful and fun for kids while they are learning. My classes combine singing, hands-on activities using instruments, and lots of movement, which make it possible to learn from lots of avenues. When we perform, we want the audience to feel something and get a message. I tell the children, "You're going to have to perform in front of other people. You may be a boss someday, or you may be making a presentation about a project. So do your best and communicate." It's a lot about teamwork. Most often, nobody goofs; they're all on task.*

The Baker School gives weight to the performing arts. Spearheaded by the principal, the school philosophy is that music and performance enhance educational experience, interest in school, and lifelong learning. Ruth teaches each class once a week during a scheduled teacher-planning period. As each grade does an evening and day performance during the year, each student has two opportunities to hone the skills of performance in front of the whole school and parents. Typically, Ruth directs twenty-six performances annually. Parents are committed, helping with sound, lights, backgrounds, props, and programs. The performances have gained such a reputation that there is usually standing room only and traffic jams in the parking lot.

> *Performances take a lot of planning and practice. I start at the beginning of the year and have a performance every other month. It takes a lot of effort, prep and rehearsals. Depending on the grade level, a performance can take two to three months. As I only see the children once a week, I'm often supported by classroom teachers, who help with practicing using a CD that I provide. Each performance has about one hundred kids and includes well-articulated standards-based materials that incorporate music, drama, and dance. I also make sure that content area standards are included. This year we focused on patriotic music because there's so much involvement with national elections.*

Ruth has the unique challenge of integrating the performance arts standards with all of the different grade level standards, so she makes it a point to communicate with teachers at each grade level to determine what units of study are being covered. When multiplication facts are being studied, students come back singing multiplication songs...or songs about geography, or parts of speech. When students are reading *The Island of the Blue Dolphins*, they create and act out skits based on the book. "Ruth's knowledge of music, drama and dance, combined with her energy, commitment, and love for teaching enable her to create integrated music lessons that capture the attention of her students from the minute they walk into her classroom until the lesson ends," states her Principal, Collette Zea.

> *I like to create lessons that give all children a chance to expand classroom concepts, so I make sure there are lots of connections with other disciplines. I do keep my*

eyes and ears open in order to be aware of what teachers are doing; sometimes I go to grade level meetings to see what's going on with curriculum and how teachers are handling content. For example, I recently saw a second grade teacher at recess, who asked me, "Do you have a song that teaches the passage of time? Our kids will be tested on the concept." (Typically, I'll research to see if a song has already been written, or else I'll write one myself with words to existing folk songs and rhymes and sometimes to my own music. I especially love to do this as I see it as a challenge and feel honored that my subject area can support teaching.) So, I wrote a verse during recess, and I gave it to the teacher to check and make corrections using her buzzwords and concepts. I added more verses for the following week. Not only did kids sing it, but they played instruments too, using rhythm sticks for the beats. They timed the verses watching the clock, tested different time variations, and easily learned the concept.

I found out that fifth graders were learning about atoms and chemical elements, such as oxygen, zinc, and carbon. I asked the teacher if she would like me to compose a song, and she gave me a textbook about what her class was studying. A couple of boys, who usually come by my room to help me, asked what I was doing and offered to help me write the song. I found that I needed to learn more about atoms and gave questions to the principal, the fifth grade teacher, and even a teacher at the middle school, who checked the lyrics for accuracy. When my helpers suggested that we arrange the lyrics to the tune of "The Adams (Atoms) Family," I knew we were in sync. It was a great joint effort! Success is when I see the kids nodding that they like the song; they absolutely love it!

Ruth makes sure that she includes students who have special needs, and she makes each child feel special by building self-esteem through music, dance, and drama. Classroom teachers recount examples of countless youngsters who may struggle academically but flourish in her classroom. One student had physical disabilities that made it difficult to participate in a dance performance with other students. The solution was to have him carry flags representing the countries of the dances, and he beamed as he walked across the stage. Another student was quite shy and had a learning disability, which made daily class work a challenge. Yet she was able to sing a solo beautifully during a performance. Her confidence soared, and she went on to perform again at the school talent show. Ruth takes the time to learn about her students, asks questions of teachers, and finds ways to get to really know students.

This year I also have two special needs classes, grades one through three and four through six with about eighteen children each. It's a joy to work with them. Although most have learning disabilities, the children can partake in performances, and they are mainstreamed with their grade levels. All children have their own special learning styles, so using a variety of different methods to teach plays to the strengths of the children. When my third graders were learning to multiply by threes, we learned to "feel the threes" by conducting in three quarter time as a conductor would, making triangles in the air. Then we went on to move in threes, by learning to waltz. I occasionally opened my classroom up during lunch or recess, and on many days there were fifty to sixty children waltzing instead of playing. Students have fun learning by standing, sitting, lying on the floor, verbalizing to a partner, using pantomime, jumping, skipping, walking or hopping while reciting, singing information, using puppets, and even leading the instruction.

Ruth implements innovative extracurricular opportunities for students. She created the "Baker Singers," comprised of forty fifth grade students, who perform at school, district, and community functions. Ruth coaches them during lunchtime; the students would rather sing and dance at lunch than play outside. They brought their Broadway style of music and choreography to the Moreland Board of Trustees, performed at many community functions, and sang at the regional Goldin Foundation Educators Forum.

> *I believe that it is important to work hard and go for your dreams, and I want to ensure that students have opportunities to shine by performing in the school and wider community. It's been an amazing to see the students, who come from two different schools, befriend each other through the Baker Singers. Their enthusiasm touches the audience. Our repertoire consists of pieces such as "Relationships" and "We Are the World," which are positive pieces that exhibit good morals, character, and values through the lyrics. What I want to instill in my students is that they can reach out to the community, to the world, just by using their gifts.*

"You rock, Mrs. Mathewson." Students, in addition to parents, fellow teachers, administration, reflect on her abilities to motivate and inspire students. "She gives them a voice, she gives them choices and respect, and she treats them like adults." "I have never known a teacher who can motive children to learn more than Ruth Mathewson." A devoted former student, Elaine Perkins, wrote, "It has been over seventeen years since you last taught me, but I have some of my best elementary memories from your classes and performances. You always made the class fun, whether it was playing some kind of game using imagination, or learning how to sing the states in alphabetical order. You have touched countless lives before and after my class. My life and the world would not be the same without you."

I was inspired by music during my childhood. I had a cousin who played "Ragmop" on the piano. I remember listening to him when I was in third grade, and I was enthralled so I started piano. In fourth grade, we had a music teacher who picked kids to play different instruments, and I was chosen to play the lone triangle. He visited our school again, and for some reason I was chosen to play the triangle again. That did it for me! I also participated in choir, but as I was afraid of my drama teacher, I chose not to be in plays. However, as an adult I did take a drama class, and realized that being in front of kids all day long, I'm an actress after all.

Ruth reflects on her teaching career and shares her personal visions for the future.

It's been thirty years, and I still love it. I am excited that our school district values Performing Arts and what they can do for children. Even though it may not be a formal period such as I teach, I would encourage all classroom teachers to try to have a music curriculum and spend as much time as possible in the instruction of the arts in ways that integrate academics. Music and the other arts touch people's spirits, offering them unique experiences to express themselves and enjoy their individual and collaborative creations. I have read that the highest academic achieving schools in the United States are spending twenty to thirty percent of the instructional day on the arts, with emphasis on music. I really believe music and the visual arts could better academic achievement.

I would love to see much more money allocated for education. In California, we are facing millions of dollars of cuts next year and much more the year after that. I learned, during a recent trip to Costa Rica, that their government spends more than twenty eight per cent of the national budget on primary and secondary education with a ninety-three per cent literacy rate for people ten years and above. They have made schooling a priority with money that was formerly wasted on war efforts and is now spent to educate their youth.

I value professional collaboration, and I appreciate the feedback of fellow colleagues who have guided and encouraged me in my teaching. Most teachers want and need encouragement and direction; they need to know if and when they are reaching children and making a difference. It's also OK to take risks and learn from your mistakes. Watching other teachers, whom I admire, has shaped me as an educator. Although I wanted to be a music teacher since the fourth grade and truly believe that I am doing what I was created to do, when I actually started teaching, I didn't know a thing about discipline. Frustrated with the children's behavior, I would end up yelling to get them quiet. As I observed other teachers, I noticed that the most wonderful teachers had gentle yet firm control in their classrooms. Their expectations were clearly stated. They didn't threaten, humiliate, or lose control of the situation. I got some advice from a teacher, who was a mentor to new teachers, who told me that she states her expectations of good behavior to children, praises them when they do well, and reminds them when they need to improve. When children misbehave, she tells them, "That behavior is not appropriate," or she questions them about their choices. She keeps her eye on her first graders, and she "nips it in the bud," when she notices the beginning of a behavior that might indicate a student is about to make a wrong choice. Many years ago, I taught at a middle school where I was upset by a few children who walked into my class late every day. I would tease them, plead with them, or give them tardy slips, but nothing worked. One day, as the latecomers walked in, I ignored them and told the others how much I appreciated them for coming in on time and how much I respected their good character and work ethic. From that day on, I put more energy into praising good behavior rather than bad. It is a simple lesson, but I had to learn it.

So I pass on some advice to new teachers: Scan the classroom constantly for signs that the children comprehend and are interested in what you are saying. At the same time, watch for good behavior and praise your students specifically. As some people say, "Catch them being good." Maintain high expectations of your students in behavior and academic achievement. Teach them that there are no limits to what they accomplish.

As we all know, the arts are always the first to go when the government has to make budget cuts. As a music educator, I've learned first-hand what music education means to children. They absolutely love it, and they enjoy its many creative outlets. Letters, which I've collected over many years, have proven time and time again that music enhances a child's enjoyment of school and is an effective tool to use in the instruction of all academic subjects. Numerous studies prove that music education makes children smarter by improving memory and both reading and math scores. Some parents have told me that their children struggled to learn certain concepts in math until they learned songs to help them understand, memorize, and remember. I would love to see all children have at least two periods of art education each week. Let them sing, dance, move, create, and have joy while learning! Ask children if the arts are important to them and if they'd like more time learning them during the school week. I know what they'll say.

Ruth is willing to share her songs with others and can be contacted at: *rmathewson@moreland.k12.ca.us*

෴

Beacons of Light: Special Learners

Stephen Kusisto, in his inspirational book *Eavesdropping: A Memoir of Blindness and Listening,* talks about "seeing light with the inner eye." He is blind. He sees by listening. He travels around the world and discovers the art of sightseeing by ear. Thirty years before schools attended to the needs of special learners, Stephen's parents encouraged him to be inquisitive and explore his surroundings without supervision. As a child, he reclaimed his world of blindness by the use of touch, heightened listening, and visual descriptions by his companions. He is now a fully involved adult engaged in writing and speaking to others about his philosophy of life and experiences (Kusisto).

How shall we attend to the needs of special learners in our schools? Full or partial mainstreaming? Personal aides for the severely challenged? The questions are open for discussion, and possible answers are shared by several teachers recognized for excellence, who exhibit expertise in working with physically, mentally, and emotionally challenged children; English language learners; and students at risk. These teachers display a passion for what they do and have amazing facility for helping children emerge out of the shadows, navigate unfamiliar environments, and find their own pathways of enlightenment.

ॐ

Sharon Taylor, 2006

Children with many different needs, talents, and interests achieve in her inclusive kindergarten classroom.

There are children who come to kindergarten ready to read and write, and there are those who don't know the letters of the alphabet. A vast majority of the students in Sharon Taylor's kindergarten class comes from low income and socially disadvantaged backgrounds; some are non-English speaking; and others have physical, emotional, and learning disabilities. All of them come to pre-kindergarten and kindergarten needing a good and trustworthy adult role model and experiences that will help them in school. Sharon is a beacon of light to her early childhood students at Crosby Kindergarten in Crosby, Texas. First as a pre-kindergarten teacher for five years and then as a kindergarten teacher for six years, she creates an academic environment that allows all of her students to be successful.

> *I love the positions of both pre-kindergarten and kindergarten teacher, because at these early levels children are already at risk for being successful in school as most of them come from environments that are not conducive for success. I feel honored I am able to create an environment where each child can be successful, one that is nurturing, loving, patient, kind, and disciplined and also promotes self-confidence and risk taking.*

When her school district officially adopted an inclusion philosophy for educating students with disabilities, Sharon enthusiastically volunteered to integrate them within her classroom. At this early level of schooling, mainstreaming special needs children with disabilities such as autism, ADHD, mental retardation and emotional disturbance creates considerable challenges. Yet Sharon focuses not on their labels, but rather on what they can do.

I really enjoy teaching special needs children. It is amazing to see their progress when included within the regular education classroom. I don't think of my special needs kids as being "inclusion" kids. I never feel they are different. They have the same behaviors; they just might need some modifications in their academics. I treat them the same as I set both high expectations and boundaries for all the children. I reward everyone for their good behaviors, (not focusing on the other), and I make a "big deal" about their accomplishments. At this age, when they get positive reinforcements, it's enough for them.

Typically, kids at this age are very accepting. Five years ago, we had a child in a wheelchair, and the students helped to set up the room to make it safe. During times when we've had children who have emotional and behavior problems, the kids, when asked, respond truthfully about what they see. They just want to know "What is the deal?" I tell them, and then it's over. We don't keep everyone asking...we just say what's what. Last year we had an inclusion student who was autistic. At times, he was in his own world...moving, shaking, clicking; and some of the kids started mimicking his actions. I talked with them when he wasn't there in a matter of fact way. The students asked good questions: "What?" "How?" "Why?" I told them that some of his movements make him feel safe; and the kids accepted this. It became OK for him to move around the classroom even though the rest of the students stayed put. The kids even helped him with his reading and blending of letters.

In kindergarten we have discussions about how to be good citizens and how to treat our friends. Children are given a voice, and the goal is for each child to articulate what is happening, how and why. The focus is not on tattling but rather on telling...in plain words, what happened, how it makes you feel, what might we do differently...and that's the end of the problem at hand. They know that this is our school family.

Crosby School District defines its inclusion model as placement of children who have been identified as having two disabilities, such as autism, speech impairment, language impairment or physical challenges in a traditional classroom. In pre-kindergarten and kindergarten, children are tested in order to get them ready for learning early in their schooling. They might be pulled out for individual attention fifteen minutes twice a day. In first and second grades, special needs children are included within a traditional classroom and are pulled out for "labs" for focused academic tutoring. Since grade levels are grouped together around hallways, there is a plan for having a floating aide for several classes. Other children might also get this specialized attention if they are slower learners or not developmentally ready.

My own preference for inclusion is to have no more than two special needs children within a classroom with one teacher. Any number above that requires having additional adults, which leads to the potential of a chaotic and certainly less effective classroom. This is especially true if the children have emotional and/or behavioral challenges too, which requires a different level of attention. When a teacher has too many inclusion kids, she loses out and so do the other kids. Yet, I feel the inclusion classroom is a bonus. The traditional children act as good role models for the special needs children to emulate. Our children's growth is so huge during the kindergarten year. It's great if they know a few letters and sounds and have started blending them. This year most of my class is actually reading!

Everything from the arrangement of Sharon's classroom to her lesson plans is designed with the success of each individual student in mind. Learning centers and small group meetings give students opportunities to work at their own levels, and Sharon praises the small steps and accomplishments, not just the final product. Her approach is to give her students the structure needed to be successful while allowing them to be their own persons. She is firm, fair, and consistent. She defines her expectations, and students know that even when they can't stay on task or "mess-up," Sharon cares for them. This extends to greeting students as they enter the classroom, lots of hugs and praises throughout the day, and snacks for those who didn't have enough to eat before coming to school.

Sharon provides cooking activities, makes learning games, reads stories that teach students about their environment, and works with each child on socially acceptable behavior.

My goal is for children to have fun while they are learning. There are so many creative ways to teach concepts with skills. When we studied dairy cows, we made ice cream. This activity led to writing recipes, following directions, and learning why and how liquids can change to solids. When we made gingerbread cookies, we compared where children took their first bites—legs, arms, or head—and made a graph. Children also iced their cookies after following the directions.

I really like having multiple learning centers, a concept that for some reason is not as much in vogue today as in the past. It's important to play and work and at the same time learn about social skills and exercise verbal skills. Children learn from each other more than they can learn from me. For sure, I don't have a very quiet room, which doesn't bother me at all. The children are moving, talking, and fully engaged.

At the learning centers students work in pairs. Typically, when students have finished their group work, they check a wall chart, which prompts them to go to a center, usually several times during the day. The chart has wooden pegs with their names on them that are regularly moved so that students will try out different centers with their accompanying skills and activities. Our students get to be very independent. I use this time to work with a small group of two children on necessary skills such as learning shapes or number recognition. Examples of our current learning centers are:

Playdough: involving counting and fine motor skills

Art: using buttons, beads, yarn, and markers to experiment and manipulate

Writing: making books and drawing

Computer: learning games chosen to reinforce concepts

ABC: matching letters and words

Blocks: being an architect to create towers and even stages and benches

Lego table: using fine motor control to create shapes

Being "Teacher": using a pointer to go over shapes, counting, weather graph, tooth graph and other visual aids

Library: quiet reading

Home: pretend cooking, dressing up to emphasize cooperation and other social skills

Math: manipulatives

In Sharon's inclusion kindergarten classroom, a great life lesson of acceptance is taught to her students. (Upon entering her room, one is unable to identify which student might be one having a learning challenge.) Sharon expects no less of these special education students than she does any of the other students in her class. As a result, unbelievable strides have been met, and her students are achieving. A parent volunteer notes, "I've never seen anyone have so many nice ways to ask people to give a little more effort. Always so positive, Sharon has a way to make children think they can do something they never believed they could. And guess what, they can do it. They can't help giving it their best shot. They would do anything to please her. She raises the bar of expectation, and time after time, and they rise to the occasion. She is patient always. Without exception, she is kind and courteous, influencing in her way, and somehow they think it was their idea and a good one too."

I have been exposed to some exceptional role models: those who believed in my educational success, set high expectations for me, built my self-esteem, and encouraged confidence and self-discipline. These teachers always took time to make a difference in my life. In junior high school, I decided I wanted to quit band; however, my band director, Mr. Vidrine, knew exactly what to say to keep me from being a quitter. I learned from him the importance of continuing no matter what obstacles you face in life. Another influential teacher was Mrs. Alexander, who taught ninth grade English. She expected only the best from her students; it did not matter who you were or what background you came from. She took extra time with me to build my confidence and self-esteem. She recommended me for the National Honor Society and encouraged me to attend a leadership camp in Colorado. She always made me feel the sky was the limit. Because of her encouragement and support, I went on to become Vice President of my senior class as well as be involved in a variety of school organizations.

"Sharon is a doer," stated her principal, Ronnie Davenport, "one of the rare people who not only has an idea, but combines this with the commitment of being actively involved. She is a member of the campus inclusion team; she is involved as a member of the district-wide committee to review curriculum, programs, and make suggestions for changes. She takes a lead in raising money in two campus fundraisers for cancer and for the district's very special needs children."

A gifted educator, Sharon molds little minds of preschoolers who are ready and eager to move on to first grade. She instills in each one a genuine love of school, learning, and acceptance of others. She is their teacher, their friend, but most of all, she is their advocate as they begin their journeys in school.

> *Working with special needs children has made me more creative and definitely more innovative. I believe that these children will do what you expect them to accomplish within reason. I do not focus on their labels; I focus on what they can do. The hardest thing about being an inclusion teacher is when colleagues look at your special needs children and comment that next year there might not be a teacher that will put up with him/ her. I cannot and do not worry what a teacher will do next year. My goal is to educate and help each child reach his or her potential.*
>
> *It is clear that I found the perfect job. I believe my most significant contribution to education is being involved in an inclusion program. I have a certain connection to these children who are at such risk for failure. I want to give back what I was given...a chance for each child to learn and succeed. Children do not have a choice in which environment they are born, but as a classroom teacher, I can and will create an environment where each child can learn.*

೦ಿ

Patrick Daly & Allison Renna, 2005

These high school teachers "turn on" English Language Learner students to writing and feeling successful.

Light bulbs flash in the minds of students in Patrick Daly and Allison Renna's English classes at Waltham High School in Waltham, Massachusetts as they make connections. Using bright colors to highlight elements of word usage, style, and composition more fully engages students, who are under-performing or are learning English as a second language, in the practice of good writing. *Writing with Colors* helps students increase their confidence and success, evidenced not only on the Massachusetts Comprehensive Assessment System (MCAS) Test, but also in their other writing and learning activities. Rather than lower expectations for students, Patrick and Allison have raised the ante. The impact has been so significant that the color criteria system has been replicated from its original summer academic support program to weekend programs and classes during the regular school day. The writing process has now been adopted school-wide as an instructional approach for all Waltham High students, from English Language Learners to special education to honors level students.

The unique, creative, and seemingly simple method uses a color criteria system that relates colors to the basic elements of student writing. Students use one color to shade the thesis/topic/focus element of their composition while using other colors for each of the following composition elements: transitional phrases, commentary/analysis, and supporting details. Both the students and teacher can immediately visualize the main elements in their composition. After seeing a few of these colorful compositions, students are better able to organize future compositions.

> *It started out as a Title I summer program in 2003 for remediation in Language Arts and Math. We got a grant to teach reading, comprehension and writing to ninth*

grade kids who failed the MCAS in eighth grade or were recommended by their teachers. The population consisted mainly of English language learners and included special needs students, kids having reading comprehension at the seventh grade level, and underachievers.

This was a big deal for high school kids! Just imagine coming to class for four weeks, one and a half hours each in Language Arts and Math. You're not confident with your vocabulary, and you don't understand certain literary terms because you never were exposed to them in your native language. It's eighty-five degrees and you're melting. You're not fluent in oral English let alone written English, and you'd rather be somewhere else, preferably a pool. One could feel the resistance as these forty kids, who were divided in two classes, weren't taking the summer program seriously. On one of those very hot days, we were analyzing open response paragraphs on the whiteboard, and we asked a student to highlight in color the topic sentence. Then we asked others to highlight supporting details in another color, and then others to color the explanation. The students were out of their seats and moving around. They were grabbing markers to assign colors to different parts of the paragraph; they had to consider what the "job" of the sentence was, and they had to justify their answers. They truly were in the moment!

There's a lot of fear about taking the state test and passing it in order to graduate. ("I'm trying to fit in a new culture and a new nation, and I have to take a high level test.") We tried to put ourselves in our students' shoes. We spent time getting to know the kids, encouraging them to talk about their fears and frustrations. Our fo-

cus was on community building, talking about cultural differences, and playing vocabulary games; and then we gradually attempted the English passages. We established trust and gave our students more confidence so they would be less afraid and more empowered, saying to them, "If you put in the effort, we'll help you by giving you the skills you need."

We prefer to get students in ninth grade so they can have a shot at the tenth grade test. If not, they can be retested again two more times. With better understanding of what the test consisted of, the expectations in writing, and lots of practice of the skills we are teaching, they can "do it!" And so we even meet with the English language learners after school and on Saturdays, and we've continued the voluntary summer program. Kids are now motivated to come because they can see more progress.

The success of the system is that it can be used with students having differing writing abilities. For English language learners, the colors serve as mnemonic bridge between their primary language and English. Students use the colors at first to construct their compositions, and then during the revision stage they use colors to analyze and make improvements so that their writing has well-developed ideas, supporting details, effective transitional works, logical organization and greater fluency.

Our English language learners often aren't literate in their own languages. There was a kid from Guatemala who had minimal English and lots of gaps in translating words and concepts from his native language to English. He couldn't remember "blue," but he could hold the blue marker. We've got many students from

Mexico, Guatemala and Haiti, and others from China, the Congo and other places. They may not have the literary terms, but they can see patterns of details supporting main ideas and other relationships.

"Show, don't tell" become our watchwords. We start by analyzing open response paragraphs and later long compositions, but first we look at examples of writing in the different categories such as "Needs Improvement," "Proficient," and "Advanced," so students can see what is expected. They have no clue of what the test consists. We were encouraged to show concrete writing examples by our Director of Language Arts, Tom O'Toole, who came from the state Department of Education. He was very familiar with the different levels and the nuances between them, and he was enormously helpful in helping us to further our own knowledge of the standards.

With our students, we look really closely at these "anchors" or models using the color system, which we codified, so that students can be consistent in their analysis. Our students begin to see that they can expand their thinking and justify an answer by writing a few more sentences. They learn that it's more than length that counts. It's topic sentence, and transition words, and a flow of ideas that support the thesis. Soon students begin writing their own paragraphs and show their understanding of the sentences by coding them in color.

Our students also become critical thinkers! Looking at test examples of the different categories, they compare their work: "Mine is closer to Paragraph #3;" "Mine is closer to #4;" "I definitely could have included more green (more details)." The students take their self-

editing more seriously. They're engaged in thinking about their work, deconstructing their own paragraphs, and discussing what they need to improve. They'll even grade their work according to what they compare in the anchors. What is wonderful and what is OK is that they need to see it and discuss it! Peer evaluation is also part of the process, which goes way beyond noting spelling and punctuation. Students allow others to highlight their work by looking at its organization, flow, and argument. A typical comment might be, "There is no red (thesis/main idea) flowing through the composition," or "The writer is off topic."

Writing with Colors extends beyond remediation to regular classrooms, and the color criteria system has been credited by the Waltham Schools administration as being the major contributing factor to the steady increase in English Language Arts MCAS scores to the "Proficient" and "Advanced" levels in both grades seven and ten. It is no surprise that other teachers have been extremely receptive to learning the new writing approach and adapting it to their curriculum, such as the eleventh grade research paper. The system has recently filtered down to grades four through six.

Kids get this color criteria system. It becomes a great tool for elementary and middle school students, especially when the colors are used consistently throughout the grades. In eleventh grade classes, kids expertly use blue in their compositions for noting "commentary." They look at their composition to see if red, which denotes "thesis/topic/focus," ends at just the topic sentence or flows throughout the paragraphs. Is it "routine red" or "rockin' red," they might ask as they look at style and better word usage. In honors class, they might be working on differentiation of "boring blue" vs.

"brilliant blue" as they're writing essays on "To Kill a Mockingbird." Each student is able to self-check as to whether the composition is too vague and needs more analysis.

A typical concern of any "method" of writing is that students will lose their creativity or unique voice. "Writing with Colors" is not about creating cookie cutter essays. Although it encourages and even demands that the elements of good writing be included in the essay, the manner in which each student accomplishes this is still unique to each individual. Students may use entirely different examples and details; they may select different topics to discuss; they may have a completely different analysis than a classmate in an essay; and they certainly are likely to incorporate style in their own ways.

The Massachusetts Curriculum Frameworks support schools to "encourage action research in which teachers seek to answer critical questions about teaching and learning through focused study and application of new ideas in the classroom." Creative and innovative in their approach to teaching, Patrick and Allison set high standards for themselves and their students and then work hard to see that they're met. They constantly broaden their own knowledge, hone their skills, and share what they've learned with their colleagues.

We had a great collaboration creating a course for sophomores in our school. With the support of our director, we train all new ninth and tenth grade teachers so that they can replicate the process. It helps to have a director who is enthusiastic, who also "sells" the concept! There's been great respect and communication with other departments, especially ESL (English as a Second Language) and Special Needs. We encourage teachers to come to the Saturday classes. They both hear about and see the success stories. Teachers respond to analyzing and using the "anchors" that we've provided, as they and their students can better understand the various levels and their differences.

We'd love to see our approach incorporated within the whole school system. Kids could "think color" and have a common scaffold for writing. The "Writing with Colors" method has shown to create clarity for students; it's certainly an approach that allows students not only to improve, but also do so more efficiently.

The impact of their innovation reaches out beyond Waltham. Patrick and Allison have disseminated their work with the color criteria system to other teachers at statewide conferences, and they provide professional development to other school systems. They offer their insights about their approach and teaching.

The feedback has been awesome! We've started a website for other schools to tap into. And we'd love to develop workbooks for teachers and students to have at their fingertips. There's a little frustration for publishing the work, as many of the anchors we've used aren't considered public domain. We'll have to spend the time and effort to get the materials we need. (Patrick & Allison)

There have been several criticisms of our "Writing with Color" approach. Some teachers consider it to be a "formula," and they're resistant. But we've got steady and great results, and we can encourage them to be mindful that kids need to jump before they can fly. We can build on the basics and then move on to more creative writing. Another question is whether this method is "teaching to the test." However, we've demonstrated that students can become better readers and writers starting from wherever they're at and progressing to the next level or beyond. As for the English language learners with their limited English skills, we need to give them supports whenever and wherever, like going over the facts vs. the myths of MCAS, letting them know what the test consists of, and gradually moving them from short answers to open responses and then essays to long compositions.(Patrick & Allison)

Kids know right away if you respect them. They respond to consistency and our care about them and knowing that "we're all in the same boat." Isolation is difficult; knowing that they're part of a community helps. I've found that by sharing my life stories—and I'm open with my flaws and strengths—and wanting to learn more about who they are develops relationships and gains trust. Taking the time to say, "You don't look great today. Is something wrong?" lets a student know you are in tune with him as a human being. Having high expectations (I'll get the best out of you!), respect for differences, and the right touch of humor resonates. I find that connecting their lessons with what they do outside of school is a great motivator, such as a favorite TV episode or discussing how a novel like the "Scarlet Letter" applies today. (Allison)

Teaching can be very solitary. We need to create a community of sharing, which good leadership can foster. It's always great to be able to ask questions of colleagues and share best practices. Whatever it is that works needs to be communicated, and this is so help-

ful for junior teachers as well as veteran teachers. If I research and then try something, rather than keep it to myself, I share it with others. The next day I might find in my mailbox a lesson that I might adapt. I don't view this as cheating or copycatting, as I apply it to my own personality and class. (Allison)

We're a work in progress, and there's always room to improve. There is need for opportunities to observe as well as have others in your room to observe. This goes beyond evaluation by an administrator. It's extremely important to take the time to be reflective and share the observation with colleagues. We even like kids to be evaluators, to write progress reports about us. Sometimes the words sting, but they make us really reflect and consider other ways of reaching and teaching. (Patrick & Allison)

Teaching is a living thing; it can't be static. We need to be fresh, to try new avenues; there's no one answer in one book. Teachers need to be empowered to create. When you've created ideas and lessons, you can take ownership of them. For example, we've sometimes used technology as a tool in our writing process—computers to highlight words, phrases, and sentences. It's another interactivity event that excites kids. (Patrick)

Patrick Daly teaches English, Media, and Screenwriting classes at the Television Studio at Waltham High, working with students to develop creative and innovative media projects. He has been a teacher trainer for the academic support program and a program coordinator for the middle school after school enrichment program called "Mall Mania." Patrick also spends his "spare time" writing novels and screenplays.

Allison Renna taught English at Waltham High for five years, and she has worked for three summers in high school academic support programs. She's been an active teacher trainer for the color criteria system and served on a curriculum writing study group to develop instructional approaches that incorporate the color criteria system. She's currently a stay-at-home mom but manages to keep her hands and mind in education by tutoring and teaching "Writing with Colors" workshops at other schools.

Their peers describe Allison and Patrick as "emblematic of those un-recognized teachers who deserve not only an acknowledgement for the important work that they do, but our trust, our support, and our thanks."

ℭ∾

Deborah Henry, 1993

As director of a regional alternative high school, she provides challenging academic instruction, guidance, and individualized support to students.

> *There was an eighth grade girl who had such high anxiety she couldn't function in middle school. She would go and then leave to walk home for three miles. When she came to the TEC School for an interview, she wouldn't come into the office. Many days we couldn't get her out of the car. She would stay in my office for a chunk of the day, and gradually she would attend a class if I stayed with her. We gradually weaned her from her mom, who at first stayed in the office, then went upstairs, then went to another building, and finally stayed at home. The student stayed with us five years. She became a National Honor Society member. She's at college on a Presidential Scholarship awarded for good grades (an acknowledgement of the fine work our staff has done); and she aspires to be an English Teacher in an alternative high school. We've given her the opportunity to do her pre-practicum with us. She is a great success story!*

Deb Henry serves as Director of the TEC High School, a regional alternative high school providing challenging academic instruction, guidance, and individualized support to students from TEC communities and some non-TEC towns in the Boston area. She was recognized for her consistent professionalism: establishing fair and compassionate limits for her students, supervising staff, and relating effectively with referring personnel. Through her efforts, students who are experiencing turmoil in their academic school experiences because of internal and external struggles become responsible agents in the learning process. Deb counsels and creates programs for students with varying abilities by assisting each one personally in setting realistic and attainable goals. She and her staff serve as wonderful role models, demonstrating dignity, care, and empathy. As a result, students gain self-esteem. They make contributions to their classes and schools, and they develop critical thinking and problem solving skills necessary for life-long learning.

"TEC High School in Newton, Massachusetts provides secondary students with high level academics and interactive experiences while helping them overcome academic, emotional, and personal issues which have interfered with their past school experiences. It is a supportive, structured, nurturing environment that allows students to receive a personalized education. Students in this program gain self-confidence and renewed motivation, begin to establish positive study habits, and develop successful patterns of functioning so they can succeed in school and post-graduation. Field experiences, adventure/challenge activities, and wilderness expeditions allow for the development of problem solving skills, group bonding, trust, and improved self-confidence.

Emphasis is placed on a structured college preparatory support program compatible with Massachusetts Frameworks and MCAS expectations. Students receive diplomas of their sending high schools. There are curriculum offerings in English, Algebra I and II, Geometry, and Advanced Math including Pre-calculus and Calculus, United States and World History, Criminal Justice, Biology, Anatomy/Physiology, Zoology, and electives including languages, physical education, and career internship options. Dropout prevention is established by providing a community based environment where students historically achieve academic and personal success" (The Education Cooperative (TEC) website).

It seems like there's always been TEC School. It started thirty-two years ago with fifteen kids in grades 9-12.

*Now we serve 35-45 kids that also includes grade 8.
I attribute its success and longevity to a number of
things:*

➤ *TEC School is unique in whom it serves. We're a college prep
school that takes in kids who can handle academics and engage in traditional classwork, but likely have some emotional
overlay that hinders their activities. Our students are not really
severely learning disabled. If one comes to us with an IEP (Individualized Ed Plan) for special needs, we'll never say "no"
but take a good look at his/her issues. Our kids have lots of
different interests and talents, which we try to harness, from
computers to science to the arts. What they have in common
is an emotional overlay of anxiety, depression, family trauma,
or outside crisis that affects their learning in a mainstreamed
environment.*

➤ *Kids are moved from the larger high schools to a small school
setting. They need to be out of a building where the sheer size
of the place and the number of people can intimidate them. Our
kids, who likely have high anxiety and depression, have trouble
being in hallways during change of classes; there's too much
going on in the cafeteria; and some can't handle being on an
open campus site. A school in the midst of being built creates
too much hubbub and confusion for them. TEC School recognizes their need to be in contact on a personal level throughout
the day with lots of acknowledgment. They are getting a fresh
start from teachers and other kids. I don't think we've ever
lost that.*

➤ *Social connections tend to improve with the supports we
provide and the smaller number of students. Typically, these
relationships are negative in their home schools. Our students typically gravitate to others students who are disen-
franchised, do the least amount of work or none at all, and
skip classes.*

> ➤ *We tend to get a lot of parental support. We encourage them to be proactive and step up to the plate. We'll use our "tricks in the bag" to get parents to show up, talk with them about their responsibilities, such as helping with homework, and giving it to us straight. I might say to a parent, "I really encourage you not to cover for your kid, like really tell me that he won't get out of bed. Then our teachers and I can work with him."*

> ➤ *We do our all to support specific needs, such as following and tracking meds. We'll provide follow-though on therapy and include therapists in all our planning.*

> ➤ *There are absolutely no drugs or alcohol allowed on campus. We know that some kids will sabotage this rule, which may be indicative of emotional or social behavior to come, and we'll do what we can to support them.*

> ➤ *Kids here really trust the staff. There's consistency. There's a line to cross, and they know it. From interview day, they hear, "We need a super-safe day for kids to have and that means no toleration for anything destructive in the environment." For some kids who have never heard the word "no" before, they need to understand there's a "no" for the right reason, which is not arbitrary. The "why" of the rules or what we are doing or saying shows respect for the kids.*

> ➤ *We give our kids a sense of history, which they love to hear about. We have lots of photos and tales to tell.*

> ➤ *Although most of our students tend to stay here at the TEC School, going back to their high schools is always on the table. If there is reintegration, we work closely with the high school team to ensure a safety net. The student is part of the discussion.*

When I look back, and this is my twenty-fourth year, I realize that I have grown so much. The time doesn't seem possible; I really can't wrap my mind around it. There's so much change. Every year is different, and I still get excited about the new year every September. One of the hardest things for me is the loss of people I've gotten used to working with, be it retirement or moving to another position; and I miss them. We actually have little staff turnover, which works to our kids' advantage. They get to have a sense of expectations and even how to handle success with teachers who return each year.

I've learned some things as an administrator. I've always had autonomy and independence in my job, thanks to my executive director, which is a large part of who I am. I think that this gets the doors open and is helpful for staff. I try to pass this on. As one of my responsibilities is to ensure the continuity of the program, I reach out to many high schools. I try to do more public relations for the decision makers, the designated guidance counselors, special ed directors, principals, and superintendents. This has become even more important as there's a huge turnover of personnel in referring schools, and I am always in the process of re-education. "So, here we go. Start from scratch." I've developed a well-packaged packet of materials including a yearbook and newsletters that thoroughly explain the program, which I leave after a visit or a phone conversation. This is followed up by a personal phone call to answer questions. One of the best selling points for the program is inviting people here where they can meet teachers, see what's going on, hear a class in action. There's a pulse in here: quiet, focused, and interactive.

Age is a wonderful thing as it leads to wisdom. I'm still learning to pace myself. The school has the potential for burnout with unexpected crises and isolated inci-

dents. In contrast to my thirties when I thought about covering everything in the course of a day, I now take one day at a time and talk to myself and others about doing the best we can do. I'm better at keeping myself healthy: eating well, taking time away, spending more restful weekends, and taking chunks of time that are not work related. I feel less compelled to do all the physical activities with kids that we do, from climbing walls to rope exercises and difficult canoe and hiking trips. (I still think I'm twenty-five and actually do this stuff, but I'm more careful.) My family is a great support for me and continues to give me stability. I attribute my longevity in this job to them. It is an extremely high stress position, and they keep me grounded.

෬

Torches: Leadership

Life is no brief candle to me; it is a sort of splendid torch, which I have got hold of for the moment, and I want to make it burn as brightly as possible before handing it on to future generations.
George Bernard Shaw

We need torches in our lives, people who listen, empathize, have vision, and empower others. Striving for meaningful connections and making changes to better the lives of others can be a solitary venture; more often, it involves actively developing relationships and pursuing activities with others such as family members, classmates, and the broader community. Educators often are the first to introduce leadership skills to their students. They know that leadership can be learned and that the skill set doesn't mysteriously appear but is shaped over time. Leaders and future leaders need to learn, practice, and modify their craft. To accomplish this, administrators, teachers, and children need many direct opportunities to deal with conflict or change, contemplate choices, listen effectively, influence others, establish long-term goals, solve problems, and make decisions and evaluate them.

At times, an opportunity for leadership presents itself when it is not anticipated. Because of circumstances a person responds to a need, gets a positive result, and is moved to exercise further leadership. Greg Mortenson's journey of discovering leadership is profiled in *Three Cups of Tea.* He learned important lessons from the leader of Korphe, which is a small village in Pakistan, who said, "If you want to thrive in Baltistan, you must respect our ways." Mortenson reflected that this wise old man taught him to "slow down and make building relationships as important as building projects. He taught me that I had more to learn from the people I work with than I could ever hope to teach them." This skill was practiced repeatedly as The Central Asian

Institute, led by Mortenson, created many schools and sustainable projects from schools to water purification sites in Pakistani villages, all of which were built on relationships. Becoming a change agent, he learned how to be slow, steady, and persistent. He listened to the people who advised him, and he listened to the people who were being served. Modifications to the overall plan were made based on each village's needs and requirements. Building on a successful model, he was able to replicate it. In the village of Randa, where children weren't educated unless they could afford the cost of transportation and tuition to a private school, Mortenson worked with everyone in the village to supply the land and help build a replica of the Korphe school in ten weeks (150).

Many have written about the importance of good leadership in schools and its advancement by a strong, positive school culture in which all of its participants play roles. Principals communicate core values in their everyday work; teachers reinforce values in their actions and words; parents bolster spirit when they support the work in classrooms; and community members participate in governance. Kent Peterson and Terrence Deal describe a culture where there is a shared sense of what is important, a shared ethos of caring and concern, and a shared commitment to helping students learn. The vision is clear; the climate is consistent; there are numerous opportunities for collegial dialogue, problem solving, community building, and shared ownership of responsibilities. Accomplishments of all its participants are celebrated. (28-30) This climate has a ripple effect on students, who observe the behaviors of administrators and teachers in a positive culture and have many chances to practice the same skills.

Deborah Meier, in *Keeping Schools,* talks about laying a foundation of democracy, where people are open to the possibility that others have something important to say. They are prepared to consider each other's evidence, and they accept the idea that someone sees "truth" differently from them. She states that democracy, in fact, is hard work and takes time. It involves tackling hard issues and questions. Meier challenges us, "But where better to start its practice than by starting early in the schoolhouse?" (Meier 108)

༄

Gayla Haas & Kim Houser, 2005

They developed an Elementary Student Council so that their students can learn and use leadership skills to make a difference in the broader community.

Gayla Haas, a technology teacher, and Kim Houser, an art teacher, at Newport Elementary School in the Crosby Independent School District, Crosby, Texas, are brightly lit torches who illumine the paths of future leaders. Taking on a new challenge, they meshed their talents and energies to develop the first Newport Elementary School Student Council for the school's third and fourth graders students. Their vision is to instill leadership qualities, focus on activities that build positive character traits, and provide opportunities for students to make many significant differences in their school and home communities.

These two highly creative teachers serve as role models and leaders for students, with whom they establish a wonderful rapport. They care so much about what students do and who they become, and they always look for the good, the positive, and the best in every child. Gayla and Kim quickly responded to their principal's inquiry about starting a student council in their school, and they established guidelines for participation. Typically, student councils operate at secondary levels; yet, some groundwork was laid with Newport's Character Development program, in which teachers and students discussed themes such as honesty and diligence. For the Student Council, students elect a representative from each of their classes to serve, based on good character qualities taken from the "Keystone Kids Program."

> *It might be a shy child, one who is not the most popular, a child you wouldn't expect to be a "leader." Our goal is to tap into each child's strengths, his/her interests and talents, and build self-esteem and self-worth. We give our future leaders lots of praise as they tackle new*

responsibilities and projects for the school; and it is
remarkable how much they grow and are willing to take
on new roles.

Kim and Gayla spend time modeling and talking to Student Council students about what makes a good leader. They take about ten of the forty children to an annual leadership workshop "Student Council Leaders R US" in the Houston area. They've even hosted the workshop at their own school for several years with their own leadership team acting as hosts. At this workshop, which is sponsored by TEPSA, the Texas Elementary Principal Supervisors Association, students and advisors learn to create a dynamic student leadership team. Students and teachers discuss leadership styles, how to network with other student councils, and they learn more about roles and responsibilities such as planning an agenda and conducting a meeting. They share strategies for generating peer participation, and they explore tools to create meaningful and challenging projects and fundraisers (www.tepsa.org/StudentCouncil).

We have learned much from attending these workshops,
lots of strategies and ideas for involving our students.
It's an intensive bonding experience. Our "take" on
it involves our student council reps in a twelve-hour
marathon, a sleepover event in our gym every fall. This
leadership event grooms forty children, who represent
thirty-five classes plus five members of the former third
grade class. Our goals are to build a cohesive group
and seed projects for the coming year that the group
decides. We first involve students in "Getting to Know
You Games," such as challenging them to" find some-
one who lives near you" or "discover who has a sibling
with the same age as yours." We put them through some
exercises that get them to think about their strengths,
leadership styles, and what kind of leaders they might

be. We involve them in setting our individual goals as well as future goals for high school and even college. There's tremendous bonding as they participate in doing activities that are laid out on mats on the gym floor for them to choose, some of which will be used for our future projects. Throughout the evening our students fill out affirmation notes (there are thousands of these pieces of paper) and put them in others' affirmation bags, which has students' pictures on them. It's wonderful to see our kids' eyes glowing, see them involved in brainstorming and planning. They are quite the creative thinkers!

Student Council members have many chances to hone their skills throughout the year. They plan, make decisions about how to implement the projects either in their own classrooms or for a full school project, make posters, and exemplify community service to other students by example. They recruit students in their classrooms to help, typically asking, "You are a strong person, will you help us?" And the quality of their projects is apparent. Often the entire school community is involved in outreach to others in the broader community.

Validation and celebration of Student Council members' efforts are part of the process. After their classmates elect their representatives, an induction ceremony is held, over which a local judge presides. Students' pictures with brief descriptions are prominently displayed on a bulletin board in the hallway. There is recognition by the community as the various events led by Student Council members and undertaken by many other students are highlighted in newspaper articles.

What Gayla and Kim have done with the leadership program and the experiences they have provided for the student members have exceeded everyone's expectations. Achievements of this group range from creating a scholarship for graduating Crosby High School seniors, raising money for the American Cancer Society (among several other organizations), and collecting school supplies for the children of Afghanistan. The Student Council spearheaded a letter writing campaign to benefit area service men and women, and they organized a food drive that stockpiled enough food to supply sixteen families with a traditional Thanksgiving feast.

Examples of additional projects:

> Student Council members hosted veterans and family members at a reception and music program honoring veterans on Veterans Day.
> Students held a mock election on Election Day. Student Council members served as election judges, registrars, and voting officials for the day.
> They frequently visit assisted living centers. At one, students sang and danced with residents during Christmas, and they also interacted with them by asking them to talk about what they did when they were children during the holiday.
> They planted yellow pansies in school flowerbeds in honor of service men and women serving our country.

By the end of the school year, Student Council members evidence their leadership qualities in many ways. They take responsibility; they understand risk taking; they become influential in getting students in their own classrooms to participate in projects; and they take initiative. In their planning process, when we ask them if they need help, they'll often say, "We've got it; we're under control. We'll ask for help if we need it." And they do know how to tackle the project and see it through!

We remember our very first student council president, a very shy quiet child, who became very self-assured as he assumed greater leadership roles. His job was to present the high school scholarships at the award assembly. All you could see of him at the podium were his eyes showing above the rim; he didn't even want a stool. But he carried on; he really showed courage, and he received a standing ovation from the crowd.

There is sensitivity for teaching leadership skills to other students too. Kim and Gayla assume responsibility for another group of students at Newport, for whom they channel students' potential leadership skills in positive directions, such as becoming accountable to others besides their regular classroom teacher and learning how to follow through on their own group projects. These students are nominated by their teachers and meet as a group and individually with Kim and Gayla. Sometimes they are paired with Student Council members.

We believe that the success of each child is important. We praise students' successes and encourage them to make better choices when they've made errors. We want them to take responsibility for themselves. We will ask an individual child, "What can you do better? What might you do to make this a better situation?" This is all a part of the learning process. We try to model and teach character building skills to all students on the campus.

Kim and Gayla are leaders by example. They serve as mentors to new teachers. They feel it extremely important to be there to provide the specifics: the how-to's of the bells, whistles, and sirens; the first phone call; the first parent/teacher conference; how to deal with all of the massive supplies the first week; how to schedule the day; and how to compose the ever increasing emails. Kim and Gayla are quick to provide affirmation and give lots of hugs.

There is never a "dumb" question; don't be afraid to ask. Remember the best; forget the rest. Ask yourself, "Will this really change my life?" If not, let it go. Learn to laugh; the lesson may not go the way it was planned. What's really important is first reaching the child with the content coming next.

Step out of your comfort zone every once in awhile, and try a new course or activity, personal and/or professional. For example, perhaps you could broaden your base in a subject area such as math, which might lead to a specialized class in probability or a Math Club. We like change and challenge, and we choose not to be complacent. Just jump in! Enjoy teaching! It's the most rewarding career that we can imagine.

We're really fortunate in that our school system supports mentoring over a period of time. We need to give new teachers support over a few years, and to this end, the district will pair them with "lab" teachers in art, writing or math, and retired teachers. We need to retain our new teachers! By the time they reach their third year, it's when things start coming together and making sense.

Kim Houser

"If you need to start an art program for over three hundred fourth and fifth graders that addresses art appreciation, fosters creativity, produces a Houston Rodeo Art finalist every year, and covers the Texas Essential Skills in all subject areas, go to Kim Houser," stated Christy Co-Van, Assistant Principal. Kim, the art teacher at NES, created the first elementary art department in the history of Crosby School District. Previously, each teacher was expected to teach art within class time. Kim now teaches every student basic art techniques and skills along with art history.

Kim eagerly shares her talents with others, often collaborating with classroom teachers and specialists such as the music teacher. She demonstrates that "art" is not merely the product of a painting, song, or dance, but rather it is a style of innovative expression that no two people will have alike. Kim creates many ideas for integrating art and literature, and she's eager to get kids hooked into reading. She will even transform a classroom to make the children feel as if they are walking into the book along with the characters.

It wasn't until fourth grade that Kim won her first art contest. She understands the meaning of diligence. Even third and fourth graders can relate to her story of trial and error, and it is through her own real life experiences that she can show them how important it is to try to do your best, not just in art, but in everything. Kim is admired for her patience with children. She is never demeaning, always soft-spoken and treats them with gentleness and kindness. She has a knack for getting students to perform well in whatever area she is working them. Finding out what they are interested in, she taps into those talents. She will find students who are lacking love and give them extra attention, checking on their progress and making sure they have everything they need.

Kim is one to take new teachers under her wing: modeling lessons teaching them how to write effective lesson plans, sharing a wealth of experience on classroom management, and motivating them when they are feeling down. She conveys her enthusiasm for writing and art, which she feels go hand in hand, both being highly creative. Her special skills in language arts and reading have allowed her to assist and lead in special tutoring in classrooms and labs.

Gayla says about her partner, "Kim is an artist. She looks at the canvas (her students) and sees the painting. She sees the emerging masterpiece: successful, confident, and responsible. Her pallet is colorful and diverse. She continues to create masterpieces everyday in every aspect of her life whether it is in her classroom, working with the Student Council of Ambassadors, a fellow colleague, or creating a new 'canvas.'"

Gayla Haas

Gayla is the leader overseeing and implementing the school's vision of technology, accounting for all of the equipment in the building, mentoring staff members, and assisting with every program at the school. As the Computer Lab instructor, she uses every opportunity to share real life applications while reinforcing the traditional disciplines of reading, writing, math, and science. She takes third grade children and very patiently and enthusiastically walks them through the basic skills of computer literacy. By fourth grade, they become quite talented, even creating PowerPoint presentations, skills necessary for success for today's professionals. Encouraging students to write and use their technology skills, Gayla also created a school newspaper. Known as the "frog lady," due to the number of little green guys in and around her classroom, which have been given to her by her adoring fans and peers, she is very popular. Gayla is the main resource, too, for teachers: troubleshooting technical difficulties, hooking up computers in classrooms, helping with computerized grade books, testing over six hundred students to find their Accelerated Reading levels, searching for websites to correlate classroom lessons, and helping children do research.

Gayla looks for the good in every situation and expects the same for her students. Beginning each of her classes with what she calls "Family Time," students share something about their families that is good which fosters interest and respect for all. She never misses an opportunity to pull aside a child who she feels needs a little extra encouragement and give him a reason for wanting to make the right choices. If children have been having problems, she will take them for extra time and help them look up things for their projects. When classroom teachers had difficulty finding time to give students make-up work in a quiet area, Gayla set up a "Stop R" room where children could "stop" in order to benefit themselves and their teachers ("Supervised Time Out with Positive Reinforcement"). She keeps it running with supplies and establishes weekly schedules for proper supervision.

Gayla created additional innovations. "We Deliver" is a writing program, which is based on the U.S. Postal Service that encourages students to write communications to other students. Students write to each other, drop their communications in a central mailbox; and their communications are delivered.

To help promote unity among classmates, Gayla developed the Cougar Coupon Count chart that is proudly hung in the school's main hallway. The goal is to encourage positive behavior in and around the halls of the school. Students must work together as a class to earn coupons by being examples of positive behavior and evidence "Keystone" characteristics.

There are numerous ways Gayla taps into the fabric of her community. She serves on the campus technology committee and district wide technology committee. She has presented a paper and project to her technology peers at the state TCEA Conference. Her project on weather using technology was published on the Technology Applications Teacher Network for Texas.

Gayla has certification in administration, yet she states, "I'm where I want to be."

Kim offers praise about her partner, "Gayla is a lifelong learner who finds the best in every child, loves to tackle new jobs, and is always looking for ways to improve what we already have in place...a leader...caring heart...energetic. She is a pillar of our community."

ॐ

Peggy Bryan, 2004

A talented and innovative principal, she leads her colleagues to think of creative new solutions to age-old ways of doing things.

A guiding star for her elementary school community, Peggy Bryan is cited by her colleagues as an "extremely innovative, extraordinarily inspirational, effective leader and community builder." Since 1997, Peggy has served as the Principal of Sherman Oaks School in the Campbell Union School District in San Jose, California, which serves a largely immigrant population, grades kindergarten through sixth. Under her leadership and co-authorship, the school changed status in 2000 to become a charter school; its model is that decisions are made by the teaching staff, with input from the principal and oversight by a governing board composed of various parent and community representatives.

I'm really proud of what has been accomplished at Sherman Oaks. People are still very excited about our charter school concept, which was started ten years ago and is in place and flourishing. We were fortunate in that we had a full year to plan, recruit, and build community; and this paid off in so many ways. We conducted over a hundred visits interviewing parents and others in the community about what this model school should look like on this empty field in their midst. And we wanted to be inclusive, incorporating their ideas along with our goals of a dual immersion program in English and Spanish, project based learning, and constructivist pedagogy. We knew we had to come up with quality time for staff who wanted to work systemically, and we created the concept of the mid-day block for teacher planning. We spent hours in generating ideas. Eventually we came up with a simple construct, but we didn't get there without a lot of sweat. When we first presented the concept of our charter school at the traditional district staff meeting, they laughed at us. But we showed them. We had our vision; we knew how pivotal it was to make our program work, and we did the planning that was necessary before implementing our unique concept.

Peggy is a deep thinking person, one who can interpret, analyze, and process information extremely well. She has a great vision of how things could be, and she is a brilliant problem solver in carrying out that vision. Her creative juices flow when she is working through ideas and challenges. Colleagues note that she is a mentor to her staff, leading them in thinking of creative, new solutions to age-old ways of doing things. She rarely says, "No, we can't do that." It's always, "Why not?"

I saw a poster with ducks lined up in a row. I asked myself, "Should I be the leader, follower, or get out of the way? When do I insert myself in the situation or project? How do I foster problem solving?"

I had an administrator's dream here at Sherman Oaks. When the concept of a special charter school was being formed, I spoke to many people about the possibilities. A hearty band of people stepped up, and a cadre was charged to take advantage of the opportunity. In starting the charter school, I was more of an architect. People's voices could be heard, and we created as we went along. Sometimes I was silent, sometimes I brought hot chocolate and lattes to enliven our group, and at times, I reinforced them by showing a silly movie.

My first administrative assignment was in leading a start-up alternative school within a larger traditional high school. The program was designed for students at-risk, and we needed to re-engage them. I was interning—I was cheap labor; and they didn't need a rookie. So from that point, I went into complete service mode. I did it fast and well, from running off copies to faxing. I won them over by rolling up my sleeves and showed them that there was nothing to be intimidated about, and I could be trusted. I earned my way there; these teachers and I bonded, and to this day, many years later, we are friends. I learned that when coming into a new situation, the im-mediate goal is to build relationships. This leads to trust. Then people are more apt to listen.

My learning style is organic. What's rich about Sherman Oaks is that we can take an idea to action very quickly. We have time together, which is built into the schedule to distill ideas and then plan and implement. I try not to say "no" to new ideas and, in fact, encourage my staff. I practice what I call the "How Dare You Factor." Sometimes when I find myself feeling this (and we all do this at times), it's usually a matter of ego, and I have to shut down my voice. I find this promotes healthy growth.

I think of myself as the shovel behind the desk. I shovel power to kids and to teachers. This is not done indis-criminately. I must know when kids or teachers are ready and foster enough confidence to proceed. I look for the edge...for them to gradually increase their skills. This is a dynamic process. Everyone has the capability of being leaders. Sometimes we also need to follow; this changes from project to project, day to day.

A major achievement is the creation of the Midday Block, a "win-win" for teachers and students, which Peggy helped design, support, and fund. In effect, it lengthens the school day. This is an extended prep time for teachers that fosters staff development and collegiality, be it group planning, preparation of special school events, or Spanish classes for non-Spanish speaking staff. During this period, a variety of activities for students take place: an extended lunch; running clubs, which have led to improved student fitness; and art classes taught by a cadre of professional artists. One year there was a Latin American storyteller for Drama and Art, who augmented the school's dual immersion language program, and a visual artist who taught computer graphics.

> *I believe in simple, economical programs that work. When you see what a school values, look at the master schedule; it's all there. Once you lock the program in your master schedule, you've got it secured...some tweaks, and it has staying power. For example, the original model included one day a month per grade level for teacher planning time, for which we provided subs. This involved even more planning by the teachers for the sub, and often more supervising by me. We've moved from this concept to two variations that we think are a win-win for everyone. Grades kindergarten-three teachers prefer the one-day a month plan, and for this day we will bring in four enrichment specialists in art, physical ed, science, drama and also a roving teacher for the day. The upper level teachers, which is now grades 4-6 (originally the school was K-4) prefer to have the one hundred fifty minutes a week, which means that two teachers might pair for planning...a simple, yet elegant plan.*

Some highlights of Peggy's many innovations include:

➤ Encouraging parent participation and leadership. A bilingual PACT Parents' Group meets monthly to address issues facing local families and acts to formulate and support needed programs. Results of their efforts include: an after an school program, a Healthy Kids program which is a quality low cost health insurance program, parenting classes, and a morning ESL class with child care.

➢ Sherman Oaks is the only school in the district that offers a federally subsidized breakfast each morning. Peggy also uses Title VII funds to hire a parent part-time to assist other parents in finding needed resources, be it helping with domestic violence or landlord issues.

➢ Another very important accomplishment at Sherman Oaks was one year's one hundred fifty-three point increase in the school's academic performance index, the largest increase of any school in the state. Part of this accomplishment can be attributed to Peggy's hiring of a coach, who worked with teachers individually and in groups on how to improve the reading and writing of students.

I'm most proud of the close partnership we've partnered with PACT, which is an activist, progressive, faith-based community activist program that is designed to develop organizational skills to meet needs expressed by community members. They are asked, "What bugs you around here? Who wants to do what and how and when?" You should have seen our PACT reps presenting their points of view to people at City Hall. When the question of renewal of our charter school for another five years came up, parents were rallying like mother lions. Spanish parents spoke English and English parents spoke Spanish as they presented their positions as a group to the school board. I loved their energy and give and take. It was great!

I convey to my students, teachers, and parents, "You are special. Change the world. When you leave here,

> *remember that you are a representative of Sherman Oaks." If I could make changes, I prefer a K-8 model, which helps to keep kids as kids longer and protects them during this most vulnerable time. I also prefer a small high school instead of the big comprehensive high school model where students could opt into schools that specialize in certain subjects and activities...basically dynamic small focused schools of choice.*

Peggy left Sherman Oaks to study full time at a seminary. Nevertheless, she served as a coach for the incoming principal for one year, was gone for a year when she interned in Oaxaca, Mexico, and then she came back to Sherman Oaks to share the responsibilities as principal for another year until a new administrator came on board.

> *We are fortunate in that the new administrator speaks Spanish fluently and comes from a similar culture as many of our parents. Her challenge will be to win the confidence of parents who perceive themselves different from her. Already, she is proceeding proactively, having had three meetings to better know our parents. We helped set up these meetings, as we know from experience that our parents tend to like more formalized groups and committees.*

> *After I graduate from the seminary, I will be working as a parish priest in a large geographic area for our Episcopal diocese. I want a church without walls, a "charter church" that might meet in a ball field or under a bridge. We have a new bishop whose working theme this year is "Year of Wonder," and in fact, her theme for next year is "A Year without Walls," so we're in sync. I will have freedom in my own parish to implement the ideas that we want.*

I hope I can bring a little piece of Sherman Oaks to my new position. My immediate goals are to build relationships and develop trust. The ideas for developing "community" are important. I'd love to have the kids who go on mission trips do more than fix and build, important components to be sure; they could spend two weeks living with families and learning about the culture.

∽

N. Jerome Goldberg, 1994

He significantly influences the quality of education for children by empowering the school staff to take charge of their professional development.

> *I believe strongly that we develop Teacher Leaders who have high expectations and standards for increasing student performance and raising the bar. Teacher Leaders carry the torch because administrators unfortunately have to spend a lot of time doing everything other than "instruction." We have to empower educators to develop their skills, train them, and give them opportunities to deliver the goods.*

Jerry Goldberg understands the flame of potential, and he encourages children and adults to aspire and shine. He brings a unique perspective to professional development based upon his varied experiences as an educator. While serving as an Assistant Superintendent for Instruction in the Natick, Massachusetts Public Schools, Jerry empowered the school staff to update their professional development, which led to a powerful infusion of ideas and teaching strategies that rippled down to students. As Superintendent of Schools in Natick, he used his knowledge and experience to work with and enlighten a variety of constituencies: teachers, parents, and members of the community. As a former elementary teacher and reading specialist, he identifies with the needs of a classroom teacher. A college professor, he brings his practitioner's knowledge of educational theory to students entering the field of education and energizes those who are currently educators. Currently a consultant for Teachers21 in Massachusetts, he continues to inspire educators to take charge of their learning, supports them in the process of exploring new instructional approaches, and develops professional learning communities in many school districts.

*What ultimately happens after training our Teacher
Leaders is that we get a built-in mechanism to work
with others. We did this in several ways. I taught an
in-house course on "The Skillful Teacher," based on
the highly recognized concepts and practices of Jon
Saphier, which eventually became the criteria for continued employment in Natick. All new teachers took
the course, and teachers whom I trained helped in this
process. Another model involved hiring outside professional development teams to teach courses such as "Effective Writing Strategies" and "Effective Math Strategies." Several teachers who took each course then presented it to new teachers and supported them throughout the year with coaching and monthly workshops. We
also handpicked teacher facilitators who worked with
grade levels. An entire kindergarten culture was rede-
signed, because based on their expressed interests, we
provided teacher training and empowered our Teacher
Leaders to lead the charge. Our Teacher Leaders were
recognized and compensated.*

Jerry used his own course of professional development and pursuit of
advanced knowledge in addition to his base of teaching administrative
experiences to develop different forms of professional study groups.

*I was fortunate as an administrator to have had the ex-
periences of teaching first and second graders. I sort
of knew how to work with young children as well as
older students. When I pursued a doctorate in Reading,
I learned more about language acquisition, which always fascinated me, and the use of multiple modalities
to reach young children, which I used successfully. I was
an administrator at the time, and Marie Clay, the guru
on whole language development from New Zealand, was*

presenting her work at a conference. I came back very motivated and established a study group that focused on "Early Childhood," which met once a month, and now, twenty years later, still meets. The group convenes at someone's house and studies together, looks at research, has guest speakers, visits each other, and implements their ideas. The state of Massachusetts has allowed us to use this in-service time towards recertification, and teachers love the collaborative learning.

I think study groups are one of the futures of education. They are phenomenal and targeted learning communities and so influence some of our practices. I'm a catalyst. I've learned that it's more about empowering people! In Natick, we established a study group option that encouraged professional educators to research specific topics of their own choosing. Ten different groups formed. Each had to present a proposal, meet its purpose, keep records, and note their accomplishments. One high school group looked at Level Two students, the ones who are unmotivated, cause problems, prefer to sleep, text their friends, and do everything <u>but</u> be highly engaged in their studies. They are not "special needs" with regard to physical or learning challenges. The study group came up with some excellent teaching strategies that promoted student achievement.

Jerry designed the Mini University program, which encourages the staff to earn graduate equivalent credits with improved teacher effectiveness and collegiality as direct results. Courses included "Non-violent Intervention," "Discipline," and "Cooperative Learning." Jerry taught some of the courses himself, which included: "Understanding Teaching," "The Idea Factory," and "Multiple Intelligences."

I was fortunate as an assistant superintendent that I could teach courses. They were non-judgmental and never took teachers' issues personally; rather, they were positive from the viewpoint of "How can I help you grow?"

I had read about Motorola University, an in-house group that transferred the authority of professional development to leaders, who were trained. With the support of my Superintendent, I started a Mini University for the Natick Schools with the goal of establishing professional learning communities and changing the school climate. I liken some professional development efforts to an air freshener—smells good for a few minutes but doesn't have a lingering effect. If you use a plug-in, it constantly infuses. With our new model of professional development, we could empower leaders, set high standards and expectations, and take a very focused approach for the future. Then we could use building blocks to spread the knowledge. All of our actions are geared toward increased student performance and self-esteem. Anyone, from teachers to secretaries to janitors, could come in and ask for support as long as it was practical. It also had to have a good theoretical base. Then together we would look at "How can we do this? How can we manage it?"

Jerry has had a trajectory of experiences as an educator.

I was first interested in psychology. I was looking for a position when I heard that Lesley College was interested in hiring a male to teach special needs children. Well, I did have camping experience and loved being with kids. I took the position and got a master's degree in Special

Needs, which launched me. I started teaching special needs youngsters in Melrose, Massachusetts. I always had the philosophy of integrating all children within a traditional classroom unless there was a full school designed to meet their needs. Teaching gifted children also became an interest, and I hooked up with Bernice McCarthy for a summer program and then became a trainer. To this day, I still work on differentiation of education teaching strategies and applications so that teachers can meet the needs of all students.

What really shaped me as an educator is that almost everybody I worked for empowered me in a number of ways. When I was teaching first grade, I was the only male in early education in my district, and somehow my students were getting the highest scores consistently year after year. The facts were that I was getting a doctorate in reading, had experience in special ed programming, and was creative. I've been mentored by great people at every phase of my career. All were very strong and demanding but extraordinary. I learned from them and mentored others.

My Superintendent, Joe Keefe, and I, in my capacity as Assistant Superintendent of Curriculum and Instruction, made a big effort to support teachers. Initially we did an intense screening of teacher candidates. We also reviewed all teachers with their building principals and visited every classroom every year, and we looked at an individual's strengths and areas needing improvement. I've learned that it's vital to pick the right people, set goals, and give them lots of support and the straight scoop of their performances. They need to be accountable. Sometimes this means that an administrator has

to cut losses. If I could have made a change in my ca-
reer pattern, I would have also had the experience of
being a principal. I think being a principal would have
enabled me to put a lot of my beliefs in one environment
with a common core.

Under Jerry's guidance during his tenure as Natick's Assistant Superintendent of Curriculum, the elementary evaluation system was
reviewed and revised. There is now a focus on various assessment
strategies, resulting in a more holistic view of a child's achievement.

I believe in accountability. Assessment is linked to
learning, not only the final analysis, but also pre and
on-going assessment. The cumulative effect works; it
changes the focus. To all my students, administrators,
teachers, and children I offer the challenge: "What can
we do to raise the floor and eliminate the ceiling for
others?" We don't have to pile on more and more of the
same. We need to empower people to do the best they
can do.

Jerry has served as an adjunct faculty member at Lesley College as
well as Simmons College. He is affiliated with the Saphier Research
for a Better Teaching Center, belongs to a number of professional organizations, and is past president of the Massachusetts Reading Association. Teachers21, where he's a consultant, is a non-profit organization focused on systemic education reform that serves educators
in New England and nationally. The group's vision is that all students
will have knowledgeable educators who believe in them and work in
schools with strong cultures of professional practice. Jerry and other
consultants offer professional development for pre-K-12 that is research-based and very current; they work to improve public policy
and the public discourse through dialog with legislators, business and
community leaders; they work on policies such as teacher prepara-

tion, licensure, recruitment and hiring, supervision and evaluation, and teacher leadership.

> *I'm enjoying my work with Teachers21, where I'm start-ing my eighth year. It's a most dynamic organization that has topnotch consultants and offers a consistent message, demanding curriculum, and approaches that serve contemporary needs and issues in education. I see many ways to solve problems, which helps me in my work and allows me to see lots of possibilities. Based on the needs of the school systems, I present one-day workshops and longer courses. I spend half my time with teachers focusing on "Differentiated Instruction," "Building Professional Learning Communities," "Lit-eracy," "Assessment," and "Project Based Learning." With administrators, I might be doing "walk throughs" together: coaching on training and supervision of staff, examining what's happening in classes, and consulting on "Closing the Achievement Gap" and "Professional Learning Communities." I'm often invited back, and there's a high level of trust. In one school, teachers en-couraged us to videotape them for use with others; this was seen as a valuable learning experience.*

It's clear that Jerry is committed to sharing the wealth of what is learned in professional learning communities. He believes that there is success in each of us, that leadership can be learned, and opportuni-ties for passing the torch of leadership should abound.

ꙮ

Beams of Light: Community

We can nourish ourselves if given the freedom and love to do so, yet we also need to be nourished by others. Nineteenth century poet Walt Whitman's poem, "A Child Went Forth," eloquently describes how each child is the sum of all the people and experiences with whom he comes into contact. Whitman wrote:

> *There was a child went forth every day,*
> *And the first object he look'd upon that object he became,*
> *And that object became part of him for the day or a certain part of the day*
> *Of many years or stretching cycles of years.*
>
> *...the early lilacs became part of this child*
> *...and the grass and white and red morning glories and the song of the phoebe bird*
> *...and the changes of city and country wherever he went*
> *...his own parents, he that father'd him and she that conceived him in her womb and birth'd him*
> *...and the schoolmistress...*
> *...the village...*
> *...the horizon's edge...*

Reading Whitman's "A Child Went Forth," Julia and Hannah, my granddaughters, come to mind. With this memory comes affirmation of all who shape who they are and who they will become. Their parents and grandparents have fostered their inquisitiveness and creativity, continuing to provide the imprinting applauded by Whitman's poem. Many others, who have yet to come, will leave a little bit of themselves behind with the "stretching cycles of years" of these two little girls.

Children are touched by a variety of people right in the schoolhouse. They make a difference in the ways children learn and achieve. Some adults recall the special educator or mentors who were so influential in touching their lives. It might be the school nurse, the performing arts specialist, or perhaps someone who oversees recess. Classroom teachers, who challenge their students to go beyond simply recalling facts to thinking critically and creatively despite the pressures of getting all formalized curriculum covered, are able to share some of their own passions and experiences of learning.

And what would we do without parental involvement? From tutoring one-on-one, to assisting in special programming, to sharing experiences that complement curriculum, to raising funds for art and music, parents are proving to be necessary allies in advancing the knowledge base and continuity of community in our schools. It's the collaborative effort that makes it all work.

Many outside of the schools, yet within the community, actively support education. Some are unpaid volunteers; others may have started as volunteers and through their initiative acquired grants to become paid professionals; and others may be paid educators, who feel it important to give back to the community and be involved in the school/community partnership. Raising, teaching, and nurturing children become a shared responsibility, and we recognize and thank education's partners, who disperse their unique beams of knowledge.

The following "snapshots" highlight award recipients involved with their school communities.

Philip Hernandez, 2006 *Teens flock to The Zone, an after-school program.*

Philip Hernandez, Director for "The Zone," an After School Program for Teens at the Fisher Middle School, is the driving force behind the creation of an exceptional program in which students learn life skills, build positive self-esteem, encourage leadership and team-work, and explore their creative talents. The Zone is an outgrowth of a successful collaborative school-com-munity partnership that takes place between Los Gatos Union School District and Los Gatos/Saratoga Depart-ment of Community Education and Recreation in the Silicon Valley, California region. Over 150 students are typically registered in "Teens Reaching Leadership in The Zone." It is a safe and accepted place where stu-dents have many opportunities to expand their horizons both on and off campus. A homework center with tutors operates daily. Enrichment classes such as *Jazz Band, Japanese, Speech, Art Appreciation, and Model Race Cars* are offered either before or after school. Students participate in sports, plan special activities, take weekly local field trips, engage in community service, receive leadership training, and attend an annual leadership conference in San Francisco.

Peggy Richey, 2006 *"A Friend in Deed"*
Peggy Richey serves as a parent volunteer at San Ja-cinto Elementary School in Liberty, Texas. She has a long history of service to the Liberty community as well as its schools. She is the driving force behind an outreach program, *Friends in Deed*, which provides for the important tangible and intangibles needs of el-ementary children and their families. Another school program that Peggy began and continues is *MARCH, Mentors as Reading and Citizenship Helpers*. Liberty Middle School (LMS) band and choir students work with kindergarten and first grade students to develop reading skills and serve as their mentors. In addition, Mrs. Richey recruits community volunteers to mentor

both groups of students. Several comments from Peggy's nominators include: "Her heart is for those who struggle academically and socially, and her passion is for every child to know that someone cares for them and believes in them. She is one of the most sincere, uplifting, and selfless person I have ever known. She has been such a blessing to our school and community. Her ability to motivate and encourage children with her kind voice and artistic talents is truly a gift that has blessed us all."

Eileen Moore, 2008 *"Do your personal best!"*

It's a real partnership when school and community work together to better the lives and achievements of students. Loma Prieta in northern California is a small mountain school district of four hundred elementary and middle school students. Volunteers actually support landscaping the school ground and setting up daily lunches. After the 1989 earthquake, someone even donated the land on which the new schools were built. A community center is on the grounds, where artistic and cultural opportunities are provided to meet the needs and interests of seniors and other age groups.

The community values physical education and for many years has financially supported the position of its elementary physical education teacher, Eileen Moore, who is a master in working with youth. Her motto, "Do Your Personal Best," is evidenced by the children intent on increasing their endurance by jogging and doing other physical exercise that culminates in an annual Jog-A-Thon. Everyone in the town participates from parents running beside their children to firemen who stage the traditional "cool down."

Audrey Michelson-Newman, 2000 *Children First Preschool is a "win-win."*

Developed by Audrey Michelson-Newman through a Community Partnership Grant from the Massachusetts Department of Education, *Children First Natick* provides preschool experiences for children while parents seek gainful employment. The program has improved communication, collaboration, and resource sharing among all childcare providers in the town, Natick MA Public Schools, Morse Institute Library, and the community at large; it demonstrates community partnership at its best. Audrey adds much to the program since its inception in 1966: grant funds to supplement daycare costs for eligible Natick families; family outreach and support programs for families of children birth to age three; a family literacy program with the Morse Institute Library; parenting workshops; numerous community events focused on families and children; bookmobile visits to preschools and daycare facilities; and the publication of a *Resource Directory for Parents*. A typical day may find Audrey visiting a parent at a private home to assist with parenting skills, bringing curriculum materials to a home-based provider so that children have opportunities for enrichment, and reading a book to children at a center based program. These activities complement the tasks of supervision, training, and administration of staff.

A community activist, Audrey is a key member of "Joining Hands for Peace Council," where respect, caring, and peace are taught to children and families through many projects. In addition, she supports the Food Pantry and Natick Service Council, and has proposed a fund be set up to help send eligible children to camp in the summer. At the Annual Spring Fair, Audrey enlists the help of the police department to provide child safety seat checks. Audrey's nominators characterize her as a "guardian angel." Her energy, creativity, inspiration, and diligence contribute to her mission for "Children First."

∽

Blanca Diaz, 2005

An immigrant in search of the American dream, she gives back to her community as a volunteer, motivator, interpreter, translator, and activist.

> *When you plant a tree, you have many limbs. The balance of limbs on both sides of the tree makes it strong. Otherwise the tree might break. The limbs hold up the bloom.*

Blanca Diaz, a parent/community volunteer at Del Mar High School in the Campbell Union High School District in San Jose, California, is a sterling example of an important but often overlooked community-school link. She makes positive things happen for students, parents, teachers, and administrators. Highly respected by the entire school community for her successful and supportive Spanish-speaking parent organization she inspired and continues to lead, Blanca's service to the community is wide and deep. She serves on the School Site Council, coordinates the Spanish-speaking parent program, and translates the school newsletter and all general mailings that go home to parents. She also assists by recruiting other Spanish-speaking parents to help interpret at meetings.

Born in Guatemala City, Central America, Blanca came to the United States in search of the better, brighter life promised in the American dream.

> *For me the American dream has come true. I do not only live in this country, but I feel very much part of it. I became a mother of two wonderful children. My husband and I own our home, and we also own a family business. These are things that in other parts of the world would have been very difficult if not impossible to accomplish.*

I grew up in Guatemala, and I guess that I have been nosey all my life, and I always wanted to help others. I first thought I would be a nun because I helped out in the church. I used to sew dolls made of cloth, which were given to kids who didn't have Christmas presents in small towns in Guatemala, and I even taught catechism class. I always took my five brothers and sisters to help out in the church, too. Whenever possible I volunteered to help in the school and library as well as the church. I did this as a child and as a teenager.

I live in the Burbank community, of which the Luther Burbank School District is the hub. It is in this community where my children have grown up and where we have had the opportunity to meet many wonderful people. When my children first entered the elementary school, I became part of a group of committed administrators and parents. At that time, Luther Burbank School was implementing a new parent involvement program, which eventually became to known as "Padres Con Poder," Parents with Power. Over the course of several years, this parent involvement group became very successful and eventually was honored with both county and state recognition and awards for being an exemplary parent involvement program. It was there I realized the importance of parents being involved in their children's education as well as learning about the impact that working together has in our children's lives.

Even though her children "graduated" from elementary school, Blanca continued her role as a parent leader in the *Padres Con Poder Program*. She was asked to run for a position on the school's governing board, and she became the first elected official in the history of the district who was of Hispanic origin. In addition, she was elected to the position of board president.

At Del Mar High School, where over twenty-five percent of the students are Latino, there was need for more outreach to Spanish-speaking parents. Blanca approached the school principal, Mr. Russell, in the fall of 2003 at the first Back-to-School Night to offer her assistance in helping to get the school's Spanish-speaking parent community more involved. They began meeting that fall to devise plans for improving the communication between the school and its Spanish-speaking parents and to develop programs that would help these parents feel more comfortable in interacting and participating in school activities. Blanca translated into Spanish all school newsletters, invitations to school events, and the *Student/Parent Handbook*. She also was key in assisting the school to implement its telephone attendance communication system in Spanish that goes home automatically to Spanish-speaking parents when their children are absent.

Our school is the second home of the family. Parents need to keep this in mind and keep in touch with the teachers and the activities even though their kids are teenagers. Teachers are not totally responsible and don't have to feel they are alone in the classroom. Parents who have the barrier of a different language might be fearful of approaching the teachers, but it's important to connect with them. They need to know that parents want to help in their kids' lives and that they are not doing it all alone.

When my children started attending Del Mar High School, I felt the need to continue being part of their educational process. I recognized immediately the absence of Spanish-speaking parents and understood that, as in many cases, it was the language barriers that keep parents from being involved in their children's education.

I think it is definitely worth the involvement of parents with schools from kindergarten to high school. Children need to know that you are involved and care for them. When you have a kid in third grade and you give him a kiss on the cheek, he doesn't have to feel ashamed. With your high school kid, you can show that you are proud of them. They still want to be loved. I get goose bumps when I think of my two kids who are now attending college. My son brought some friends home who wanted to interview me about how one can make a difference being an immigrant. I shared some of my stories and encouraged them to become involved and not sit around waiting for things to happen.

Blanca also has been the impetus for the initiation of monthly parent meetings for Spanish-speaking parents. Fewer than twenty parents attended the first parent meeting; now fifty parents attend these monthly events. Blanca plans these meetings in coordination with the principal, who has been most supportive of her effort. However, she's the one who runs the meetings, translates for English-speaking staff members who also attend the meetings, and conducts surveys of parents to determine agenda topics for future meetings. Some of the topics have included: introduction to school rules, processes and procedures, gang awareness, graduation requirements, college entrance requirements, and financial aid opportunities for college. A meeting was held with the district superintendent, with the entire time set aside to provide each parent with specific academic and attendance information for their children. Parents really appreciate the commitment of Blanca and the school administration as they become better able to interpret their child's individual records and understand issues of great importance that both they and their children face every day in school and in life.

Jim Russell wrote on her behalf, "I have been a high school principal for thirteen years at three different schools, and I have never had a relationship with a parent who had such a significant impact on the school environment and culture as Blanca has had on Del

Mar High School. To watch the parents' comfort level to ask questions, to volunteer, and to watch the number of participants grow has been very rewarding for me. It has also led to students feeling more a part of the school knowing that their parents are actively involved and that the school is taking a serious interest in them." Blanca has also volunteered to assist the administration with its summer student orientation. She helps all students but is a particular asset to the English language development population whose skills are limited. Her passion is evident as she dedicated long hours to ensure that all events run smoothly and efficiently while being sensitive to the needs of all families.

I have really enjoyed working with the Parenting Group at Del Mar. Recently I talked with the parents about the survey that was given to them about their communication with teenagers. I tried to convey that parents need to be open and loving with their kids. They need to convey that with rights come responsibilities. If you give something, you will get it back. Sometimes it feels that you are not planting seeds, but you are. Kids have respect for their parents because of their attendance at the class. They have said that the class was so helpful to their parents, who could even share with their children how to apply for a scholarship and college. I have tried to show that if I can do it, the rest can.

I have always said to parents that there is nothing farther from the truth that when kids are grown that they don't need us. Kids do need us. They need to know we care. It's so important to break down the barriers of language. Our parents can participate actively in what's going on at our school, and we encourage them to do even more. In this way, they can know what's going on. For example, a week before the SAT test, we discussed the impor-

tance of the kids getting a good breakfast, a good night's
sleep, and telling them when they leave in the morning,
"Do your best." They will know that we are there for
them.

In addition to the above list of accomplishments, Blanca also works part-time for the San Jose Convention Center; is a member of the Beverly Burbank Lions' Club, whose objective is to serve the community; participates in First Five, a community group which focuses on children from birth to five years; and participates in "Weed and Seed," a community group which focuses on the prevention of youth gangs, crime, and drug addiction. Bob Lowry, who introduced Blanca at the Goldin Foundation Educators Forum commented, "I'm reminded of the old adage that when you want to get something done, ask a busy, committed person!"

It's always been my belief that there are two ways to
be helpful. One can ask how to help, or one can just do
it. Now in addition to helping out at the high school, I
help in the Lions Club's efforts. I love their motto "We
serve." There are so many things that they do for the
community. One major contribution is collecting glass-
es for Central America. We have collected them in our
shop.

Blanca comments on her life experiences in the school and broader community as an active participant and observer.

Sometimes we are too concerned about grades and
achievement. While they are important, I think that be-
ing a human being, one who has morals, one who can
socialize, one who can take responsibility, is even more
important. Being the better person should be the high-
est goal as students can be exposed to good citizenship,

participation in school and community activities, and volunteerism. I tried to do this for my students when I was a teacher of shorthand in Guatemala. I taught and showed them, "If I can do it, we all can do it!"

I think that teachers need to talk to kids beyond grades. They should be alert if a kid has a problem. They need to talk with them and show them respect and really get to know them. It's important to have relationships and personal knowledge. This leads to getting kids engaged to humanity, and they learn more and faster.

I, too, focus on personal behavior. One thing I've recently done is treat and respect the humanity of people. When I walk to my workplace, I greet people by saying "Good morning" or "Buenos Dias" even when I don't know them. Just acknowledging them and showing respect has never failed to bring a response.

Our parent group continues to meet on a regular basis all together—parents, administrators, counselors, and deans, sharing the same goal of participating in our children's education and helping them to succeed because we know that together, we can make the difference. A great accomplishment for me is to be an immigrant in this country, able to do anything I want. God Bless America!

ᕲᕲ

TEC Career & Instructional Team, 2001

These caring and committed professionals developed enduring internship programs that involve thousands of students and community volunteers.

A unique concept of regional programming takes place in the western suburbs of Boston. Fifteen school systems have been collaborating in a consortium, The Education Cooperative (TEC), since the 1970s, to provide regional opportunities for students in programs that each district could not provide on its own. In addition to its primary focus of many special needs programs, the collaborative provides regional enrichment, professional development, and cooperative purchasing.

The team at TEC consists of a group of dynamic women who work part time in career development and exploration for middle and high school students and enrichment for K-12 students. Margie Glou, Fran Peters, Judie Strauss, Linda Curtis, Kathy McDonough, Joanne Billo, Jane Davidson, Elaine Sisler, and Ellen Sherman, Lauren Kracoff, Nina Greenwald, Peggy Cahill, and Deborah Boisvert take their cues from the many job-alike groups that TEC facilitates and from individual school systems and teachers. It is a difficult task to provide regional services to a group of high performing school systems, which at times can be very autonomous, and the team handles the many requests and services with sensitivity, responsibility, and flexibility.

The team is cited for innovative programs that have been received enthusiastically by students, teachers, parents and the community. The true measure of their success has been replication of some of the programs in individual TEC high schools as well as schools in other cities and states. Each initiative is thoroughly researched, piloted, and then implemented regionally. On a yearly basis, each program is evaluated and fine tuned with an unusual extended growth rate of participation and continued development.

Impact on students is considerable. The experiences in career exploration, hands-on activities, and high-level enrichment give students K-12 advanced content, choices for exploring interests and talents, skills in applied learning, and informed decision making about potential college majors and careers. Three innovative programs that involve broad community involvement and their coordinators are profiled.

TEC Internship Program, Coordinator Margie Glou

The TEC Internship Program, which started in 1979 with a pilot group of fifteen high school students, now serves more than 250 juniors and seniors a year. The sixty-hour internships, which generally takes place five to six hours/week for ten to twelve weeks, provides an in-depth, hands-on experience in a chosen field. Each student is individually matched based to his/her interests and schedule. Originally, the thought of a hands-on internship experience for high school students seemed remote, as this was an opportunity reserved for college students. The program's longevity speaks to the unique TEC program design and implementation. The program, in fact, has had several permutations: a summer internship for students who don't have time during the school year; an extended internship, which is an eight to ten hour a week apprenticeship for students who need an alternative experience and are trained by industry; and a new post-secondary internship program for students who graduate and need more time to consider options for college or working. Some of the fields that students have interned in are: *Architecture, Law, Engineering, Landscape Design, Cable TV, Journalism, Veterinary Medicine, Hotel Management, Psychology, Theater, Medicine, Finance, Physical Therapy, Business, Computer Hardware, Computer Software, Interior Design, Film, Advertising, and Education.* (The Education Cooperative)

> *This TEC Internship Program has so much value. It shows high school students the importance of education and how it is valued in the workplace, which motivates them to continue their studies. Also, it reinforces*

education, as students see the value in what they're studying. It teaches confidence by relating to adults who aren't parents or relatives. It helps them set goals for themselves before they graduate from high school. It also helps clarify a major, determine if it is the right path or whether to choose liberal arts; or it might provide knowledge that the content, style, and personality of the particular workplace is or is not a "fit."

Matching kids to their specific needs and interests is what makes this internship different and meaningful. My most unusual and challenging placement was a student who wanted to explore pyrotechnics. We placed him with a company in New Hampshire, and he did his internship during the summer. This high school junior actually was involved in Boston's Fourth of July huge Esplanade production. What an exciting experience!

Another intern spoke at a meeting I recently attended. As a television news reporter, she recently covered the presidential primaries in New Hampshire. She mentioned that the TEC Internship Program was a pivotal point in confirming what she wanted to do for her future. I was thrilled to hear her! As a high school student interested in TV broadcasting, Kim had been matched with Continental Cablevision, a local cable station in Needham, Massachusetts because of her interest in TV broadcasting. The company gave her many hands-on experiences, and she was a dynamo. She went on to the Newhouse School of Public Communications at Syracuse University, had her own TV program at Syracuse, and later worked at stations in Rhode Island, New Hampshire and MA as a reporter and broadcaster. It was wonderful to see her metamorphosis!

Margie recognizes the value of the community's role in education.

When I think of the community's involvement in making this program successful, I appreciate the commitment that people have for education and their willingness to nurture and influence young adults. I'm amazed that so many say "yes" to becoming a sponsor, which means giving up some time during the workday to teach. I think everyone has a little "teacher" in him or her, which makes this part of the win-win situation. Most of our sponsors view this student experience as an investment in the future. If educated and stimulated, these students could potentially be a future talent pool. Many also see this as part of a civic obligation to their community as they help students make better informed decisions about a potential college major or career. And also, I think the whole experience makes the sponsors feel good about themselves. They are grateful for the opportunity to give back. It's likely others may have influenced them during their teenage years.

Many of our sponsors participate in the program for several years. Just recently, I was reintroduced to a lawyer, who I realized had worked with several of our students for five years. He related very positive and rewarding memories of his participation in the TEC Internship Program. Another sponsor, the general manager of a local cablevision studio, was great at placing students in the areas of their specific interests: news broadcasting, sports broadcasting, camera work, and journalism; every year we had students at this site. Our interns do much more than filing, doing clerical work, or answering phones. Depending on the site, most experiences are hands-on with supervision. Other times it involves ob-

servation and follow-up discussion such as in a pediatrician's office, which requires confidentiality, or a veterinarian's surgical suite that needs advanced training.

A lot has changed since the program began. I liken it to when my kids were little, when they needed a lot of management and influence. As they grew older, they needed less of both. We continued to tweak the program as it grew, making changes as needed. At first, when students went on their interviews, I accompanied them. This was replaced by a student handbook filled with a comprehensive outline of tips from interviewing to time management to dressing appropriately. The role of the internship coordinator required many hours on the phone each evening following up on the students' interviews and procuring their weekly summaries. To get our leads for sponsors, we used the Yellow Pages and recommendations from friends and colleagues. This was long before the Internet. We had to zero in on matching a student and sponsor, which also involved researching where the student lived, his access to transportation, and personal schedule. It was a challenge!

It would have been great to have a four-year follow-up survey of the student interns and get answers to some of these questions: What major did you choose? How did the internship influence you? Did you do other internships when you were in college? Perhaps this research might be a goal for future coordinators.

Margie reflects on education as a continuous source of inspiration, motivation, and lifelong learning.

As a teacher, if I found an idea that I liked, it was the greatest motivation ever. If there were certain lessons that excited me, they tended to excite kids. When you see excitement in kids' eyes, it's the best reward ever.

Never stop learning because the motivation and stimulation extends to kids. When I was teaching in the classroom, there weren't MCAS exams (Massachusetts Comprehensive Assessment System), nor was "accountability" the major factor to deal with. But that doesn't mean that creativity and inspiration today has to take a back seat. There's plenty of wiggle room for making lessons creative and exciting. I can see this in my grandchildren's classes. Just recently during the 2008 election, their teachers took opportunity to talk about current events, the issues and candidates. Even with standardized tests, there's always opportunity for a teacher to be his/her own person and do his/her own thing.

To this day, Margie is a community activist, with many of her activities focused on her love of education.

I'm proud to have been one of the founding members and second president of the Needham Education Foundation (NEF), which provides avenues for programs that aren't included in the regular school budget. It's a broad based program, which gives grants to teachers for enrichment opportunities for students K-12 that supplement curriculum. Our goal was a one million dollar endowment, which gave $20,000 in grants the first year. Amazingly, it expanded to award $250,000 this past year. We also make it possible for people to make donations in appreciation of teachers. Our community volunteers continue to fundraise and take part in the grant application and review process. In granting the *awards, we consider how many students the project will impact and its possible replication in other schools.*

I also helped to start the PTC (Parent-Teacher Council) at the high school, because there was little communication between parents and faculty other than the one designated meeting a year. With my own kids at the high school, I thought, "I have no way of knowing what's going on." At first, the teachers were hesitant and concerned about interference and parents serving as "watchdogs" about their curricula. But that never was our focus. We started a Teacher Appreciation event as a way to thank our educators. The "Crafts, Collectibles, and Antiques Show" became a yearly fundraiser that raises money for scholarships. And we started a College Prep annual event, which has admissions people coming to talk with parents about the college application process and techniques for taking a college interview.

I still work for education causes. I've never been prouder of my town, which just made sure that we have an appropriate schoolhouse for our sixth graders. Designed to eliminate overcrowding, the school is actually a renovation of an existing school building that was closed many years ago. The only override to be passed in MA this year, it means more taxes, even for the majority who don't have children in schools. It's clear that our community is actively engaged in and committed to promoting better education!

TEC Extended Internships, Coordinator Fran Peters

TEC Extended Internship Program is a one or two year experience for 11th and 12th grade students which combines academics with on-site training in an industry. Students develop proficiency in fields of their choosing that they are considering for careers. This program involves work-based learning plans linked to the student's high school curriculum. The time commitment is eight to ten hours/week and is individually worked out to best mesh with the student's academic schedule. Students receive academic credit for two courses for this internship experience. They develop and maintain a portfolio, which includes regular journal entries and materials developed at the worksite. The internship helps students focus on what they need to be successful in their chosen field, which, in turn contributes greatly to their academic experience both in high school and in college and clarifies their academic and career goals. Examples include: *Automotive Repair, Architecture, Building and Construction, Business and Financial Services, Computer Science, Energy and Environmental Science, Health Care, Bioscience, Education, Retail and Commerce, Telecommunications and Information Services, and Travel and Tourism.* (The Education Cooperative)

Jill was one of those high school kids who was of the "forgotten half," the kids who were falling through the cracks and saw no reason to go on to higher education. She wasn't sure of herself, wasn't successful in academics, and was very quiet and reticent. Both she and her parents preferred her to stay at her high school, leaving for just a part of the day rather than going to a vocational high school. In this way, she could keep her social ties and participate in some outside activities as well as academics. Jill's the kind of student for whom the Extended Internship was a perfect fit.

Jill actually knew what she wanted to do, which was to work in a specific department called "Sterile Processing" in a local hospital. It's where they get the materials and instruments ready for procedures. When asked "Why," she replied, "I'm organized. It's neat and orderly and it suits my personality." Jill worked at the hospital for two years, and they loved her. Her personal growth was astounding, probably the best thing that happened to her. Her confidence grew, and she fulfilled all of her responsibilities. One amazing story was her participation in a Career Day held at the Massachusetts Statehouse during that time. She was chosen to accompany Senator Kennedy and speak about her internship experience. The success story continued with matriculation at Mass Bay Community College, and then she was hired by Norwood Hospital.

Sam was a kid who had "family issues." He was sociable and outgoing, but he wasn't doing well academically. He wanted to do construction, and we placed him with a guy who did remodeling. He appeared to keep up with all program expectations: writing summaries of the work experience, keeping a portfolio, and coming to dinner meetings with the other interns. So it was a surprise when we found that Sam wasn't showing up at the work site. This was a major concern regarding his credits and graduation, but we knew there were other things going on in his life. His high school guidance team and we gave him another chance, which was pivotal, because he saw that we all went to bat for him and wouldn't let him fail. Yet, we also learned from this experience. I gave him early and extended supervision at his next internship site, which literally turned him around. Sam was placed in an automotive shop (his choice), and he did really well. He fulfilled all of his responsibilities; he was given a company jacket of which he was very proud; he participated in social events; and his sponsor provided an opportunity for him to attend an automotive school.

In communities where everything is so academically oriented, there are kids who aren't matching up to the traditional expectations. It's our view that we need to find or create some alternative experiences so these students can still achieve. Guidance counselors are a very important part of the Extended Internship mix. In fact, the program began when a counselor from one of our participating high schools suggested that we develop a program for kids who were turned off and falling between the cracks. So our team responded and fleshed out a program with a regional team of guidance counselors that would meet the needs of these students.

Jill, Sam, and the other students who participated in the Extended Internship blossomed! This happens a lot. Kids get a lot of experience, realize success, and get the motivation to pursue an Associate's Degree after high school. They're getting great feedback about their participation, seeing what's going on in the real world, and realizing the importance of advancing their education. Most of the students felt that their education had been in a vacuum, and they didn't see the real world application. Now it all had meaning.

There are adults in the community who feel it is important to work with young people and commit themselves to taking action. They're not parents who have to express "I love you" or "You're worthy or not worthy." These volunteers take young people under their wings, give them experiences and accompanying skills that meet industry needs, and give them grounding in the particular work environment and culture. They view the internship experience as "compelling" and an "investment in the future"; and they are willing to give students time, exper-

tise, guidance, skills, insight into a career, and entrée to an experience they would never have had. Most often our community partners are people who "wished they had a program like this" when they were teenagers because they hadn't had success or were very undecided about their futures. Others had mentors who made differences in their lives. In any case, it's not a matter of a volunteer host being a certain age, gender, or even representing a certain industry. These community volunteers have a variety of backgrounds, and they are enthusiastically involved. To them it's wonderfully satisfying to see the growth of teenagers who likely would not be "just fine" without this experience. They also see the importance of training a future workforce. After two years, this kid will likely be "ready to go" with potential for being hired. For some industries it might be an extra helper; for others the experience is seen as a valuable community service effort. What is clear is that collaboration between schools and community drives success. It's been rewarding working with members of local communities for the betterment of students, and we continue to learn from each other. We recognize these community volunteers and see them as partners in the schooling process.

Personally I think every kid should do some type of internship. It may not have to be two years, but it is so valuable to find out what you like or even don't like. For the kid who says she loves medicine and then discovers that she can't stand being around sick kids, this is an important discovery. It's a great way to explore a potential career. I think the program could definitely be replicated or adapted in any high school. It does need a liaison to make it work, who interfaces with students, school, and industry. Our high schools supported and funded the TEC Extended Internship Program. Perhaps another model might be having local industries sponsoring and paying for career exploration and development opportunities.

We also developed the TEC Post-Secondary Internship for students deferring college, attending college, or taking leave of absence from college. The program, which consists of two or three internship placements in a year with supervision, also gives kids opportunities to explore careers. There seems to be a trend of taking a half-year or full year to explore interests and talents, which makes the college experience more focused and meaningful. I also like the option to participate in community service. It is a maturing process that enables kids to gain a different worldview.

I really love working with kids. It's been wonderful being part of a process which develops programs that encourage individual growth and establish a course that makes a difference in one's life. I feel great when a kid states, "I need to take more courses. Now I know what and why."

BRIDGES, Coordinator Judie Strauss

BRIDGES is a school-to-work vocational program for high school and post-secondary school students with special needs. It is designed to provide students who attend their local high schools with the opportunity for career exploration, interest and job skill assessment, on-the-job experience, and identification of a viable future career path. This community-based vocational experience allows students to experience a variety of work environments during the high school years where they learn skills and behaviors appropriate to specific work cultures that will be marketable in the future.

Special needs kids are aware they don't achieve academically and that their behavior is different from other students. Often they are astute in knowing how they are different. The BRIDGES Program gives them a chance to enhance their images of themselves. They can achieve success in a work environment with or without support as needed and be like other students. Every adolescent wants to be the same as others. The program aims to meet its goals of students having jobs when they leave school and having a comfort zone in being able to get along with the regular community.

Our program includes students with developmental disabilities, those with emotional and/or physical challenges, and others with learning disabilities. The beauty of BRIDGES is that it accommodates all of these children and tailors the process to meet the needs of individual students. Thus, the supervision by a job coach might be continuous, a weekly review, or a monthly check-in with the least amount of support.

The whole school community inter-relationship is amazing with a huge cadre of community sponsors invested in the program. Sometime they've had a family member with a disability or known someone intimately who had one, and they want to make a connection on a personal level. There are others who feel that it is their civic responsibility. And there are those who want to reach out and make the world a better place. They believe that one of their roles is to benefit young people.

Our work sites differ according to the needs and wants of our students. The Natick Organic Farm in Natick, Massachusetts has been providing opportunities for many years for kids who need and enjoy physical labor while working outside. Students learn how to collect eggs, prune trees, and gather maple syrup. At the same time, they learn about the cycle of growth during a year. Drum Place is run by a man who formerly played in the symphony. Here kids learn the different parts of a drum, how to listen to tones, and how to help assemble a drum. Supermarkets and fast food restaurants have also been great assets to the program, serving as resources for many years. We shoot for pay from our employers, but this is not always available at the non-profit worksites.

I remember one of our lowest functioning students with a very low IQ who worked at the Clothes Closet, a store for resale of clothes. Our student's job was to sort the clothes and toys and help people when they came in. A grandmom wanted to get a toy for her grandchild, and our student asked how old he was and then pointed to an appropriate toy and said, "This would be good for your grandson." The woman later told us that the child loved the toy. Our student had some great people skills, yet she needed attention in redirecting herself back to task and organization involving counting beyond ten and sorting. How astounding it was that she could make the match!

I definitely think this BRIDGES experience is valuable. Our special needs students have exceeded their teachers' expectations. They are exposed to new skills. They also learn about different work cultures, how much they can joke, whether they can be manipulative, and how to function at company parties. I'd love to see more of a social network for these students while they're in school and later. So many are isolated; they come home and go to the TV or computer. They need friends and opportunities to socialize.

Luminaries and Legacies

If each one of us could leave the world just a little better than when we came into it, we would serve humanity. This is not a novel concept as many groups, religious and secular, reiterate the need to become actively involved. Bill Clinton, in his book, *Giving: How Each of Us Can Change the World*, writes, "Every problem in the world has to be dealt with piece by piece. There are so many ways to give. Whatever your income level, whatever your age, skills or availability, there's something you can do. If you can change one person's life, you've done a great thing." I agree. We live with others; we share common rights and responsibilities; and we can commit to leaving the world whole and wholesome for the next generations.

Everyone can make a difference. Even I, as an average citizen, can make a contribution. In 1989, I envisioned the Goldin Foundation for Excellence in Education as a small family foundation that would be a hands-on local initiative, serving as a model for making a small, yet important difference. Involvement included partnering with schools, which resulted in a lasting shared commitment. One of our goals has been to set an example for what ordinary citizens can do, beyond great wealth or publicity or fundraising, to establish a living legacy. I think it important and valuable to take on a meaningful project in one's lifetime as opposed to waiting to leave a financial bequest or even making donations, although there is considerable merit to these choices of philanthropy, too.

Active involvement creates a certain wonderful dynamism (and an increased flow of neurons during retirement, as a side benefit) when challenged to plan, interact with people, and evaluate the project's activities. I view my legacy as being involved in a giant ripple effect that occurs when someone is recognized and validated for his or her impact on kids, colleagues, parents, and the entire school community.

The award recipient is both reinvigorated as a positive force for more children and motivated to continue exceptional work. Each serves as a wonderful role model who can attract others to the profession as well. Creating a foundation is a wonderful family initiative. It brings every-one together for a common goal and shows children in the family that anything is possible while instilling the importance of giving back to the community.

The following three educators are ones their students will never forget because of their passion, their sincere and dedicated interest in them as individuals, and perhaps their influence in changing the course of their lives. In addition, they created additional living legacies beyond the classroom involving young people. And so, we celebrate them and share their unique ways of leaving the world a little better place.

∽

Eleanor Donato, 2007

She magically interweaves geography, current events, multi-cultural awareness, and giving of self to others.

Have you ever wondered at the beauty and magic of a beautiful tapestry? There's a shimmering array of threads of various hues, each one making a singular statement while forming cohesion with delicate pairings or groupings in bold swaths of color. Eleanor Donato, a grade 6 geography teacher at the Watertown Middle School in Massachusetts, magically interweaves geography, current events, multicultural awareness, and giving of self to others. Recognized for her academic projects, service for students, mentoring support for new and pre-service teachers, and many projects for community outreach, she has created a number of living legacies. Her peers comment, "She has nurtured decades of Watertown children and teachers, and her acts of giving have touched thousands."

Nominators chorus the way Eleanor personifies "community." They comment that she is "an invisible thread that weaves through a school to make it more than a place for transferring knowledge—one that draws people together in support of one another. Though this thread may be unseen, it does not happen without design. Creating an environment where children are nurtured requires a great deal of effort and care. It's more than standing in front of the class and lecturing."

> *A teacher takes an active role in her students' lives and the community in which she teaches. To truly educate the mind, you have to be willing to educate the individual, and in order to educate the individual you have to give of yourself by showing that you care more than just about grades and homework assignments. You care about who your students are as people, and where they may go in life, and how you can help them achieve their*

goals. This kind of support can't be measured by stan-
dardized tests, yet can make all the difference in chil-
dren's experiences.

Eleanor's students long remember her. Her son Brian, who is also a teacher, comments that long before he had his own classroom, he learned what it meant to be an educator. Throughout his upbringing and education, he saw first-hand what his mom did to become a valued and respected teacher. "She always was considerate of her students and went to great lengths to continue educating herself in order to develop unique and exciting activities for her students. She showed me that to truly connect with your students in order to make a difference in their lives, it is important to take an interest in who they are as individuals outside of school. Even now, she often attends sporting events, recitals, plays and other extra-curricular activities and will wait around to congratulate her students. (The looks on their faces when they see her are unforgettable.) In a more serious situation, when a student loses a family member, she attends the funeral or wake, and at times arranges for food to be brought to the family's home. And when she recognizes that a student comes from a family with little resources, she's quick to provide school supplies or gift certificates to help ease any burden with great subtlety."

Eleanor further notes the importance of sharing professional and life experiences of her students.

The one other thing I am passionate about is mentoring
student interns and new teachers. It is very important to
get involved in all aspects of the school and community.

Eleanor enjoys donating her time and energy to fostering strong relationships among everyone in the school, parents, and members of the community. Facilitating the school student council and school-community service program, she develops students' leadership skills and sets an example with three direct activities. *Pennies for Patients Drive* raises money for the Leukemia Lymphoma Society of America. Eleanor brought this program to the school while its community was grieving the sudden death of a young teacher to leukemia. Under her leadership, fundraising efforts have brought the students and community together through a series of events, which led the region in raising funds to fight leukemia and lymphoma. Watertown Middle School is one of the top five schools in the nation participating in the program, raising as much as $20,000 for research.

The whole school is involved in outreach under Eleanor's leadership! During the annual *Turkey Drive*, each homeroom puts together a basket complete with all the fixings for a traditional American Thanksgiving dinner. The leadership team distributes these baskets to residents of Watertown who are new to the country or struggling though hardships. The third project, *Coats for Kids Drive,* is a regional program. Again, this activity became a school-wide event with old outerwear being delivered to the school and Eleanor and her students delivering them to a local cleaner to be cleaned and distributed to those in need.

As a geography teacher, Eleanor is very successful in interweaving knowledge of the world and its regions, weather, and resources with current events. She motivates her students, who come from a wide variety of places and represent many different cultures, to become highly involved in classroom and school activities. One innovative activity is an annual "World's Fair," that has becomes a school-wide event. Each student in Eleanor's classes is assigned a country and asked to prepare a visual presentation highlighting the demographics, geography, and culture for that country. The project culminates with a community-wide open house during which the students showcase their presentations. The fair is orchestrated with care; parents, students, teachers, and others in the community love to attend every year.

Our curriculum introduces students to the five themes of geography and the tools of geographers. We then look at the geography and culture of Latin America, Europe, Africa, and Asia and hopefully Australia using what they have learned. We use mapping to introduce physical geography. Then we focus on human geography to understand the cultures of the world.

We tap the cultural diversity of our own community and share the various heritages within our classes. Along the way, I focus on current events so students are aware of the world around them. As we do our community service projects, I try to connect them to what we are learning. For example, "Coats for Kids," elicits the need to adapt to our cold winter climate and what happens when people do not have the means to adapt.

Eleanor Donato was inspired to give her Excellence in Education monetary award to New Orleans a year after the wake of Hurricane Katrina.

I am a firm believer that we need to share with others what we receive. I spent five days of my spring vacation in New Orleans. My sister is president of a small girls' school that serves students grades 7-12, predominantly African American students from the greater metropolitan area. Last year after the devastating hurricane, three schools, Xavier Prep, St. Mary's and St. Augustine's, worked together for the January to May term. They called their collaboration the MAX. It is an amazing story, and this year each school re-opened. I gave my sister my award, to be used as a way of recognizing extraordinary teaching, to which my husband added funds to increase the number of Excellence in

Education awards given. Three teachers at Xavier Prep were recognized for their achievements in the face of so many challenges. It meant so much to them! Sr. Eileen Sullivan, President of Xavier, responded, "As you can see, your award to Eleanor has extended to the city of New Orleans, which is striving to rebuild. Our children are our primary resources for the future. Our teachers are essential in building the youth of the future...well-educated, motivated, and equipped to handle present and future obstacles. Our award recipients typify such quality teachers. Thank you for indirectly rewarding them."

There are many educators who would choose not to work with middle school students, who they say are so absorbed with themselves and what others think of them that they are flighty, unable to absorb complicated information, and are ultimately selfish. Perhaps they need more educators like Eleanor Donato, who revels in the age group and witnesses and harnesses their boundless energy, enthusiasm, and talents because they are vested in activities that are meaningful.

ↄ∾

Dianne Langley, 2005

Using contemporary song lyrics, she makes connections between history and current issues.

In Dianne Langley's *Advanced American Studies* class where students recently staged the Sacco and Vanzetti trial, several came to school in three-piece suits and one decided to put transcripts of the trial on the Web. Students spent several weeks researching the trial, writing legal briefs, and interviewing witnesses. Then over the course of several days, they assumed roles and conducted the trial, which was adjudicated by the school's law teacher. The "AAA" class's trial did not end the way the real trial had. Through their hard work and deft debating skills, students managed to free Sacco and arrest Vanzetti for the crimes he committed.

Dianne Langley, social studies teacher and department chair at Natick High School in Natick, Massachusetts, has been teaching for twenty-nine years. She currently teaches *United States History* and *Advanced American Studies*; the latter is an honors level course she created for seniors. To experience one of Dianne's *Advanced American Studies* classes is an adventure in exciting and enriching teaching and learning. The student-centered course focuses on current American issues. It requires in-depth research, critical thinking, and creativity. The class incorporates debates, trial reenactments, historical novels, position and editorial writing, and seminar discussions. During a visit by a Goldin Foundation Advisory Board member, students put aside their group work on mini debates of various national issues in order to analyze several songs from a new curriculum resource that Diane is writing, *The Lang Book: A Collection of Contemporary Song Lyrics for Use in Social Studies and English Classes.* In preparation for the class discussion, students researched psychology books, "right to privacy" laws, and reality television. They listened to the songs several times and then had a lively discussion connecting American literature, history, and culture to real life, current issues that impact them. The valuable interdisciplinary lesson involved much critical and creative thinking. Clearly, students felt safe to speak frankly in front of their peers. Dianne believes strongly in helping her students find their voices and support their opinions.

Several nominators commented that Dianne shares a kindred spirit with their own favorite teachers. She possesses wonderful qualities as a human being and teacher. Dianne is easily approachable. She expects great thinking from her students, and she respects them. Her classroom lessons focus on authentic learning; they are creative; and they are most certainly memorable. Dianne has a palpable connection with her students. They feel respected because Dianne speaks to them as adults.

In 2005, Dianne presented *Rock on: Using Contemporary Music to Make Cross-Curricula Connections* at the New England Conference for Social Studies. The workshop spotlighted her *The Lang Book: A Collection of Contemporary Song Lyrics for Use in Social Studies and English Classes*. This curriculum resource of contemporary songs along with interdisciplinary lessons is designed to elicit information and discussion. The goal of her project is to get teachers and their students excited and interested in social studies topics through the innovative use of song lyrics in the classroom.

> *Contemporary music provides a vehicle for making historical issues more relevant as they can be understood within the context of current expression and current issues. Using song lyrics can provide a non-traditional approach that generates student interest in the lesson, uses multiple intelligences, and helps students retain information. In my book, I've developed a series of lessons that are formatted for teachers' use with specific topics and general themes. The lessons allow teachers*

to make cross-curricula connections and encourage students to understand events, past to present. Teachers can select appropriate questions and activities for their classroom. The intellectual discussion and analysis presented for each lyric can be a springboard for lessons that can be short or very comprehensive as the teacher sees fit.

My earliest inspiration to use songs to make relevant classroom connections was my son, who used to email lyrics of songs he liked. He suggested that I check out the words and the band, and I got a kick out of the fact that he thought I was cool enough to share this with me. I still stay current with music, capitalizing on my daughters' interests and asking my students, "What are you listening on your iPod?"

It is my hope to publish a book that focuses on the use of various forms of contemporary music as a vehicle for understanding social studies concepts. It will give teachers suggestions for interpreting lyrics, questions for discussion, and other connecting activities such as use of primary source documents and research that tie in with curricula. It will be awesome!

As Chair of the Natick High School Social Studies Department, Dianne, in addition to her administrative duties, mentors, provides curriculum resources, and inspires the ten other teachers in the department, most of who are new to the profession.

I was mentored when mentoring wasn't a concept. My social studies department chair and principal so supported and believed in me. They encouraged me to take risks and attempt new projects. I try to do the same for my colleagues. When a teacher in my department had the opportunity to take a sabbatical and travel around the world and create amazing curriculum replete with photos, film, and stories, I supported him. I want to give him and all teachers in my department every advantage to share their experiences with other students and teachers.

What I presently see is the heavy focus on standards-based teaching as well as curriculum driven by mandates. Core concepts, content, and skills are more than just lists to be checked off. I think it important to give my students and colleagues numerous opportunities for critical thinking and creativity. There is tremendous opportunity to capitalize on all of our individual talents, interests, and experiences.

As a curriculum leader, Dianne continues her legacy. Collegiality and expectation of excellence are part of the culture of her department. She instituted a curriculum/sharing best practice program that is a part of the weekly meeting. For her, an important focus is engaging students so they really want to learn. One initiative involved putting up banners in the hallway with inspirational quotes from famous figures in history. Students continue to bring them up as conversation pieces in social studies classes (Everyone has a favorite.), and they also appear in lessons of other academic departments. Another example for motivating students in social studies is an annual Speaker Day event. Community members having experiences in the humanities come to Natick High and share their experiences with students. Guests have included Peace Corps volunteers, veterans, law professors, and community activists.

Dianne and her family have established a non-profit foundation, the "John D. Langley Foundation," in memory of her nineteen-year-old son who died in a tragic accident.

John was an unusual kid. He was the one who would sit with the kid at the cafeteria who would be alone. He likely would have gone into social work as a career. Through our foundation's activities John's spirit lives on, reaching many young people.

I actually used some of the Goldin Foundation's format in developing the program. School personnel in several local towns are invited to submit grant proposals that identify a student having financial need, who could benefit from remedial, enrichment, or supplemental programs that their schools typically do not provide. These might include music lessons, dance lessons, a vacation week enrichment experience, or a family membership at a local YMCA. Grants meet specific criteria and are awarded by request; they are not competitive. They last for one year and can be renewed if other existing community groups such as Rotary or Kiwanis don't provide these services.

One of my favorite stories is about an opportunity given to a physically challenged youngster to attend a hospital school summer camp where he could swim and ride horses. We had a lovely note from his Dad in gratitude to the foundation as they could not afford to send their son, and the experience for his son was life changing. Another camp story involved sending a child to a 4-H agricultural camp as a diversion and help for his family where Dad was unemployed and Mom was critically ill. Mom talked about the smile on his face when he came home.

I continue to receive many letters of thanks from the families. It gives me tremendous satisfaction to reach out to kids who are in need. It's a "feel-good" effect for every-one involved. On a personal level, this foundation effort, along with my classroom teaching, is so awesome and life affirming.

Dianne Langley's nomination packet included many letters written in support of her from her colleagues, current and former students. Some comments include:

> ➤ "Dianne serves as a catalyst in the personal development of her colleagues."
> ➤ "It was Mrs. Langley's history classes more than any other that influenced me to go into the field of education."
> ➤ "I feel that my opinions matter and I can make a difference. I have developed strong opinions on issues. Before this year, welfare, the death penalty, euthanasia and other controversial issues were only words to me, but now I could debate any of them for hours."
> ➤ "She taught me never to underestimate the capabilities of students."
> ➤ "Whether you are her student or her colleague, you feel that Dianne Langley believes in you."
> ➤ "I aspire to be as innovative and creative as Dianne."
> ➤ "She demonstrates the power of education to change individual lives."

My suggestion for new teachers is: "Be authentic!" Kids want the genuine article. It's not about being the discipli-narian vs. the pal. What's important is to think about who you are and start from there. I've learned that a sense of humor is key, and I try not to take myself too seriously. The very core of good teaching is "humanity," listening and relating to your students, respecting them as individuals.

❦

Charles MacLaughlin, 2006

At-risk students in an inner city school credit him for turning their lives around.

He could have easily settled into a quiet life of boating, reading, and woodworking. He had earned much praise for his achievements at Quincy High School, where he was Director of the Heritage Program, in which many students who were "at-risk" credit him with turning their lives around. But he wasn't ready to give up the joys of the classroom. Charles "Mr. Mac" MacLaughlin, a teacher for over forty years, began to teach middle school students science, religion, and language arts at the St. Peter School in Dorchester, Massachusetts, an inner city school that has served generations of immigrant families for over a hundred years and continues to do so. With a current population of Cape Verdean, Caribbean, and Vietnamese decent, whose families face considerable social and economic challenges, St. Peter School serves as a home away from home for its students—a place where every child is known, acknowledged and loved, a small parish school that will soon be consolidated with other Catholic schools.

> *One can really get to know students in a small school, which I like. I have a wonderful opportunity to move up with them from seventh to eighth grade and a desire to instill them with a love of language and classic literature. During the process, my students learn about the world through meaningful science activities, build confidence, and are motivated for success.*
>
> *A parochial school, St. Peter's may offer lower salaries and benefits, yet it serves as a great place for energized young people who often are new to the profession but want the challenge of meeting the needs of inner city students in a high crime area. It's actually community*

service in the best sense. There is no prep time, and one is always "on." Yet, I have much freedom to seize the teachable moment, create curriculum within a core curriculum that will stimulate curiosity, and make interdisciplinary connections. I want my students to be excited and motivated about their learning.

Mr. Mac is foremost an excellent teacher in and out of the classroom. He wants to make each day meaningful and engaging for the students. Often this means thinking like a middle school student. To learn about speed and endurance, he brought in a stationary bicycle and had students bike in class. In order to emphasize distance in terms the students understand, he had them calculate the number of Big Macs it would take to get from the earth to the moon. He designs experiments and projects, plans field trips to laboratories, and invites guest speakers into the classroom to help students understand the practical applications of science.

Every moment creates a learning opportunity. After breakfast that is served in school, students enter my room to hear various types of music that refer to something going on or coming up. This serves as a point of discussion for both curriculum and values and feelings. Sometimes I use music as a bridge to allow thoughts without formal articulation. Everything on my desk is there for a reason, to stimulate curiosity. "What is that? Why is this here?" they ask. It might be a tool that will be used in a science lesson, a compass while we are reviewing the sinking of the Titanic. I've even placed my Dad's old well-used dictionary with his name on it, which once led to a discussion about respect. I love to pull experiences from my own life to help them make connections.

Mr. Mac pairs his creativity with high expectations. He deliberately exposes his students to "tough" authors, Shakespeare and Dickens, for example, so that they will be prepared for high school. He also uses films and plays, even field trips, to make these works more accessible. He challenges students to compare and contrast different versions of *Romeo and Juliet* using Shakespeare's plays and the 1960's Zeferelli film, *West Side Story.* When he can, he adds a contemporary theater production of the play when it's in town. Students memorize and recite passages from the play, dress and act in character, and then facilitate a discussion with their classmates. Mr. Mac also makes his students write—a lot! They write responses to literature, critical reviews of movies and books, and many personal essays.

> *Later in the term, there will be a further connection between language and literature when students read "Silas Marner," another great love story. Students learn how serious writers can serve as models for language and how they touch us in all different ways. They get more out of these stories when they ask questions and make connections to their own lives. One of my students remarked upon graduating, "You've taken me from crayons to perfume."*

It's the personal connection that Mr. Mac has with each of his students that is exceptional. He recognizes that what may encourage one student may frighten another away. He knows when and how far to push each student. Whether it is by encouraging one to reach for a goal and apply to a difficult high school, suggesting a list of famous movies to a student with a passion for the classics, or arranging for a student with an interest in the sciences to meet with a researcher from a local hospital, he pushes his students to discover all that they can about themselves and their abilities. They know that Mr. Mac believes in them, even when they don't believe in themselves. By recognizing individual students' personal interests, strengths, talents, and wishes while creating a trusting welcoming environment, he manages to get the best out of his students.

I like to foster a sense of continuity and confidence. I've hung pictures of my former students on the walls of my classroom, to which students often refer after hearing anecdotal stories about them. "I can make it, too" is the reaction, which is reinforced by their sense that I believe in them. I always encourage them to do their very best.

I'm always planting seeds for their future. I write personal notes and emails to students about their work: "I think you might be a great designer. Perhaps you should take a look at RISDY (Rhode Island School of Design)." I might ask, "How do I know in ten years that I will walk in your office with a broken arm?" "You could do that!" is the on-going conversation.

When I was teaching an alternative program at Quincy High School, I would give students names based on characters they resembled in their readings such as Atticus in "To Kill a Mockingbird." At graduation, I would give each of my students a book either they said they loved or one that I thought they would love. It was a reflection of their tremendous motivation and acquired knowledge to have read twenty books of great literature.

Mr. Mac reaches beyond the classroom to provide his students with experiences to broaden their horizons or supplement what he has taught. He has sponsored many field trips to museums and sections of town that students haven't traveled to such as Harvard Square, the Peabody Museum, and downtown Boston to see theatrical performances. Occasionally, he has provided students with a special trip to go fishing; in one case, he took two students to meet and watch a custom boat builder as he crafted a melon seed skiff. He has shared his family with his students, banking on their talents be it a brother's lab or another brother's interest and study of the Titanic. Over the past five years, he has even taken classes on overnight trips to New York City and Gloucester, Massachusetts. In return, his students reciprocate with affection and respect, and typically, they rise to meet his high expectations.

He goes beyond the classroom every day. He has organized the St. Peter Track Team, the annual "Turkey Trot," the school wide scavenger hunt; and every June during the final week of school, he runs the annual field day.

Mr. Mac is the type of teacher most aspire to become. "The epitome of excellence in education," note his peers, "Mr. Mac is a committed teacher, an inspiring role model, an invaluable leader, and a truly generous spirit." Mentoring others is just a small yet very important role that Mr. Mac assumes. A new teacher notes that when teaching fifth and sixth graders about latitude and longitude, she was having her students plot different locations using a graph out of a textbook. Knowing there could be a more interesting way of getting this skill introduced, she brought the problem to Mr. Mac, an experienced navigator. She says, "He immediately gave me ideas and offered to use his own free periods to teach my classes about map skills using some of his old sailing charts. The students loved this activity!"

Mr. Mac offers insights for new teachers.

> *First thing, Day 1: establish control. You're organized and in charge, and your expectation is that they will work hard. Kids need to know that this learning is serious. I never talk while they're talking or acting out. Rather I wait them out in silence until they get quiet. And, they do! Kids need discipline, and they respect follow through. If they hand in homework, they need to get*

it back with a response. Setting standards, goals, and expectations are important and can be done in a way without belittling or scaring them. If kids know you truly believe in them, they know that you're there for them even when they've gotten in a hole or have done things poorly. There's always a way to get out of it.

I think students need a change of pace. There are different ways to get at the material, be it reading, writing, or making models. I try to plan activities that make sense to them, and I tie them in with the curriculum. I even use gimmicks to get their attention. The first priority is to keep students motivated.

St. Peter School has a small staff and limited resources, and the students face many personal challenges. Few people would picture this as an ideal "retirement" destination. Yet, every day, through his words and deeds, Mr. Mac touches the lives of his students and reminds us that there is much joy and meaning to be found in this safe and reassuring schoolhouse.

If I could make some suggestions for the future of education, it would be to do what is necessary to generate excitement and motivation for learning. I wouldn't concentrate on teaching and learning to the tests, as there are other ways to also demonstrate achievement.

I prefer small schools where one gets to know his or her students well. One can give attention to individual needs and issues, even encourage kids to "make a case for it and let's talk about it." Small schools within large schools might also be an answer, and I believe the research shows that this leads to greater connectedness, community, and increased achievement.

Based on my own experience in an alternative high school program, I like the opportunity for seniors to do community service or an internship. If a student were already proficient in a subject area, I might provide an opportunity for him to take a college course.

St. Peter's may close, but I'm still ready to offer time two-three days a week, so that I can keep teaching English, science, and literature to my seventh grade kids who are moving up to eighth grade. How much I get out of teaching! I still get a thrill of hearing someone in class say, "Why that sounds like something Laertes ("Hamlet") would say," or "I heard about Lenny and George ("Mice and Men") on CSI last night."

∽

Reflections of the Author

Reflection

As educators, do we stop and reflect about what is really important? Too often in our fast-paced, period-oriented days and technologically driven environments, we are called upon to respond to countless issues and complete tasks without having a chance to review them. We need to pause, take some breaths, and reflect on our experiences of the day and year, the problems at hand, and potential alternatives and solutions for making situations even better for our students and ourselves. At the very least, each one of us can build ten to twenty minutes into our hectic schedules for some private quiet time. Booking such time into one's schedule (and this doesn't include travel times) may appear foolish, but for some, it may provide the necessary impetus for reflection. One effective approach noted for its ability to clear the head and lower blood pressure is meditation, a fifteen to twenty minute daily respite advocated by Dr. Herbert Benson of the Mind Body Institute in Boston. By regular practice of the slow breathing technique, the "relaxation response" elicits a physical state of deep rest that can change one's physical and emotional responses to stress, leading to decreases in heart rate, blood pressure, rate of breathing, and muscle tension (Benson). Whether it's meditating, reading, practicing yoga, working out in a gym, or whatever way that fosters a recharge, one is encouraged to partake in a personal "stop the world."

Our world of cell phones, blackberries, and instant messaging brings information, convenience, and instant communication. However, these great advances create their own tensions. For example, many teachers either choose or have to respond to daily or weekly emails to parents. Writing a weekly packet that goes home to parents and maintaining a class web site are other common practices that contribute to a greater workload. Often I hear about the lack of time to consider or reflect on an activity before going on to the next one, the next unit, or the race to complete the prescribed curriculum because there's a standardized test in the immediate future. It's almost as if one were assigned to read several chapters and then proceeds without allowing time to think about the purpose of the assignment, how it fits in with the subject, and what conclusions and ambiguities it poses.

Reflection can also be a shared experience. Weeks or months after a professional development experience, educators can further discuss the concepts and instructional practices that were presented. In addition, regular sessions that take place among grade levels and mentoring sessions, either informal or formal using a protocol, can be very constructive. Responsibility for making this happen most often is the charge of the building principal and school district. They need to make time for educators that goes beyond a once a semester professional development day or a period a week for individual planning. They need to promote the practice and its value so that the broader community understands and accepts its validity. When time for reflection does not occur, it behooves teachers to creatively explore ways for collegial sharing, which is further explored in the chapter "Professional Development."

Recognition is part of the reflection process. Being noticed, complimented, encouraged, inspired, and rewarded in some way promotes continued behavior. Thomas Friedman, in an article called "Behind Every Grad," describes how Williams College, in addition to granting honorary degrees, honors four high school teachers every year. Its five hundred seniors nominate teachers who had a profound impact on their lives. Williams' president states, "When you are at a place like Williams and you are able to benefit from these wonderful kids, sometimes you take it for granted. As faculty members, we should always be reminded that we stand on the shoulders of great high school teachers. We get great material to work with, well educated, well trained, with a thirst for learning." Friedman concludes, "In the age in which we live, the greatest survival skill is the ability to learn how to learn. The best way to do this is to love to learn, which comes from great teachers who inspire." And I believe the best way to ensure that we have teachers who inspire is to recognize and reward those who clearly have done so" (Friedman).

The Goldin Foundation nomination, selection, and award process involves reflection by nominators, colleagues, and others in the school community, who pause to consider "excellence" and collaborate to write a packet of nomination for an educator who has made a valuable contribution and has significantly impacted children in one's classroom, school or community. The award recipient, who is asked to share his or her projects, insights, and personal vision for education at the regional Educators Forum, must then pause and reflect in order to make a presentation. And the audience, comprised of teachers, administrators, families, parents, students, and others in the community, has an opportunity to listen and reflect upon what their colleagues deem really important. Recognition that goes beyond a certificate or bonus while also providing a public forum to affirm and share insights with others has proven to be valuable for all. Another opportunity for shared reflection occurs when I visit Goldin Foundation award recipients in their classrooms or worksites. I allow a considerable amount of time to observe each one in his/her surroundings, and then we have a follow- up time for comments and reflections. Teachers state that they rarely have had this type of experience, other than for evaluation purposes, and certainly not with time to discuss the "whys" and "hows," and they are most appreciative.

A number of themes, which I consider relevant to educators today, are further explored under "Reflections." The topics represent just a few of the many issues and practices that educators constantly reassess. Many ideas have already been presented through the lenses of the award recipients who have been profiled; additional concepts by researchers, practitioners, and Goldin Foundation award recipients, who I think have important messages to convey, are highlighted. If the reader is interested in pursuing a particular point of view, methodology, or extended research, she/he may choose to delve more deeply into the author's works. In addition, some guided questions are included to assist the reader in her/his own reflections.

◡

Power of Communication

Communication builds relationships while it transmits and exchanges information. My sense is that many people hear but don't really listen, which requires a conscious effort. Giving clear messages also includes articulation. So often we make assumptions about what the other person is thinking. I can recall many a conversation with my husband and others, and realizing afterward that we were really on different wavelengths, each thinking we understood the other. It takes work to be present—focusing on what the person is saying or not saying, being mindful of non-verbal communication, and then repeating or rewording to make sure we both are clear. As educators, I think there are several questions to ask of ourselves when communicating with students and colleagues. Do I know the needs and expectations of my listener/s? Am I being mindful that communication may vary from one culture to another? Am I being clear in thought and presentation? Am I speaking on an equal footing? Am I honoring the emotion? There is an art to listening.

In *Courage to Teach*, Parker Palmer focuses on "the learning space that invites the voices of both individual and group." He asks students to take a few minutes to reflect on the question in silence, "the silence that most students require to think their best thoughts," which is difficult to do. They then share their reflections in small groups, which gives everyone a chance to speak in a relatively safe setting. Then when the large group gathers, the voice of the individual and the voice of the group depend on the teacher's ability to facilitate discussion. It means inviting and affirming with everything that is said, but not necessarily agreeing with everything. It involves helping each person find the best meaning in what she or he is saying by paying close attention, asking clarifying questions, and offering illustrations if the students get lost in abstraction (Palmer 79-80).

We must continually hone our communication skills. One strategy is to guide our students with questions instead of answers. A number of award recipients, Lucille Burt, 2003; Jane Norton, 2001; and Wayne Chatterton, 1993, have successfully integrated cooperative groups and evaluative discussions using the inner-outer circle technique in their classes to review and analyze topics of study. One of their greatest strengths is the ability to listen to people and teach their students that skill. Using active listening practices throughout the course, these educators engage students not only in content but in the process of content. This leads to increased understanding. During the process, in which the inner circle of students engages in discussion and debate, the outer circle of students observes the inner circle students and then offers suggestions for how to communicate better using active listening cues. The experience becomes part of classroom routine, and students trust their teachers and each other enough to open their minds and hearts willingly in the circle of the classroom.

Rather than practice in isolation in our own classrooms, we can reach out to our colleagues and share our questions and answers. This requires setting time for conversations to happen, and it's got to be more than a quick pass in the faculty lunchroom or a professional development day every so often. If a school's leadership team doesn't set aside a regular block of time like Principal Peggy Bryan did, (See chapter on "Leadership."), I believe it's the responsibility of the teachers themselves to find the time to share ideas and best practices, and review a specific problem and possible solutions.

Several collegial team approaches, which exemplify effective communication, take place within numerous schools around the country (further discussed under "Professional Development"). The "Critical Friends Group," is a professional learning community that establishes student learning goals, helps each member think about better teaching practices, examines curriculum and student work, and identifies school culture issues that affect student achievement. Another communication approach, "curriculum spiraling," fosters dialog among different levels within a school district that leads to a logical sequence of content and skills.

Good news is happening in our schools, and the community needs to know it. We need to get beyond the more notorious items that usually end up as a front page spread in the local newspaper. Michael Joseph, 2008, Superintendent of Schools in Crosby, Texas, writes a weekly letter to his constituency that describes the "good stuff" that is happening in his schools, and he comments on the major issues. He is accessible to all. New technology that encourages ready accessibility to district web sites and interactive use of curriculum sites greatly furthers constructive dialogue.

Parents are perceived as allies in the home-school partnership by many of our award recipients. Some write weekly personal notes on students' work like Robin Moriarty, 2006, of Newton Massachusetts, who might comment on the improvement of a particular skill to her second graders: "Jon, you've really improved on waiting patiently while someone else is talking." "Caroline, I always notice the times you do an especially great job of staying 'unsilly' when it's your time to talk." "I'm so impressed with the fiction story you are writing. I love the way you set the scene in the beginning and introduce the characters." Weekly letters to parents and email accessibility are also part of Robin's communication package. She and other educators find keeping channels open tends to foster proactive communication.

Last, let's respect the new communication technologies but not give up on the "old"—books, essays, commentaries, in-depth conversations. There's a lot to be said for accessing information easily on the Internet, communicating in real time and in shorthand with friends, and downloading a variety of genres including music, movies, games, and photographs. It may be an age "thing," but I value the direct face-to-face with a real person in real time, the opportunity to be in a concert hall or movie theater, the holding of a book when I can physically turn the page or choose to reread a section if I so please, and the pleasure of reading a physical newspaper with morning coffee.

〰

Instruction

Who's to say what's the best way to teach? The old debates about phonics versus sight vocabulary for teaching early reading tend to resurface. Teachers question the use of graphic organizers as the be-all, end-all. There are periodic pendulum swings when it comes to education of the gifted or "School to Work," the most recent permutation of career education. I feel there are myriad ways to teach and different strategies to pursue; and while a district may dictate its preferences, there's still plenty of room for the individual teacher to bank on strengths and use creativity.

Robert Fried, in *The Passionate Learner,* states, "Every child is a passionate learner. Children come into the world with a desire to learn that is as natural as the desire to eat and move and be loved; their hunger for knowledge, for skills, for the feeling of mastery is as strong as any other appetite" (1). They continue learning at a high rate throughout their preschool years, but for some reason when they enter formal schooling, their passion is replaced by ambivalence and begins to decline (5). Fried grapples with a familiar student complaint, "This is boring." He asks, "Is this an excuse for students not to challenge themselves or to complete tasks? Are kids carelessly doing work for the sake of getting it done and handing it in because they think that getting the right answers are what their teachers really care about? Can we create a climate where students are given opportunity to take responsibility and develop suggestions for coping and ways to make learning more interesting and worthwhile?" (69-70).

Fried offers many suggestions for what teachers can do to "reclaim the promise." Among them:

> ➢ The power of "not telling" allows children opportunities for discovery and generates initiative and excitement. Children like to explore ideas, sit on them, revisit and come up with new ideas, and engage in problem solving.

> ➢ Relationships need to be nurtured among and between "teachers, students, family, and community members that affect children's pride, persistence and learning performance" (47). Teachers can't do the whole job alone but must include others in recognizing, analyzing, and combating problems.
> ➢ Teachers need to "check their attitudes" and respect their students as fellow learners by celebrating their accomplishments both in and out of school.
> ➢ A balance of activities allows all kinds of learners with different learning styles to showcase their abilities such as "good talkers, "good artists," and "good role players" (50).
> ➢ Relevancy is fundamental. All learning needs to make sense to the learners. Teacher and students should mutually engage in activities, and things to be learned must have meaning in the family, school, and community.

Fried emphasizes that the passion for learning comes from a shared enterprise for people teaching and learning together, and "that is what makes individually motivated learning possible" (261).

Here are some additional reflections regarding instruction that are worth revisiting.

Purpose for Learning

Why are we doing this? How does this fit in with what we did yesterday, and what will happen tomorrow? Do students have an understanding of what and why they are doing an activity? Educators need to take the few minutes to get their charges in a state of readiness for moving on to the next activity. It's not too different from the "preview" concept, taking a minute or two to think about what's about to be read and looking at chapter headings, pictures, words in bold, and conclusions. It's all about taking the few minutes during a writing period to note one's ideas first and then organize them in sequence before starting the first paragraph. Focus is essential. Think about the typical high school with kids rushing from one room to another between classes. Award recipient Lucille Burt, 2003, an English teacher in Arlington, Massachusetts, has a three minute meditation period before formal instruction during which students have a chance to slow down, breathe deeply, and be "in the moment" for their class. I was told that when substitutes came, students asked them to follow the routine.

Purposeful learning is based on a starting point of "What do you know?" It progresses to "What do you want to learn?" And it leads to a reflection of "What have you learned?"

⚬⟋⚬

Differentiated Instruction

"Standards, not Standardization," says Deborah Meier in *Keeping Schools: Letters to Families from Principals of Two Schools*. Not all children learn in the same way or at the same speed or age, so we shouldn't try to teach everyone in the same fashion. What we might consider is starting from what they already know to advance towards what they don't yet know. If we want them to be interested and engaged in their learning, we shouldn't purposely study things that are boring (152). Nothing turns off a gifted student more than making him do more of the same, such as completing the same worksheets as the rest of the class when he's two years ahead in knowing the material. For the child who's reading several years below grade level and lacks self-esteem and motivation, a teacher has to be resourceful to find materials that stimulate learning, perhaps books about his favorite interests.

We read and hear about the need to differentiate instruction along a spectrum of learning for the special needs youngster to the gifted student. Children do not have a choice in which environments they are born; they don't necessarily have the same readiness to learn reading at age five or six or even later; and they don't have the same talents and or "intelligences." Rather, as Howard Gardner teaches, there is a world of "multiple intelligences" that need to be recognized and actualized. Today's typical classroom is fully integrated, representing a spectrum of children having a broad range of abilities, talents, and interests. It's an enormous job for the classroom teacher but an opportunity as well. Any unit of study allows for a variety of experiences and activities that can challenge any level—from the child who learns best by manipulating materials or listening to tapes instead of total visual activities, to one who is adept at leading a small group project, to one who can pursue guided independent study of a subject related to the theme heralded by an essential question. Along the learning continuum, educators can foster self-confidence, resiliency, and independence. To meet these goals they can apply their own inspiration, talents, and tools.

There are issues of "extremism," as John W. Gardner addresses in his book *Excellence: Can We Be Equal and Excellent Too*. He cautions against two different views of extremism. One ignores differences in native capacity and achievement, which Gardner feels doesn't serve democracy well. It means committee rule, the individual smothered by the group, and it means the end of striving for excellence, which has produced mankind's greatest achievements (18). The counterpoint, he suggests, is extreme emphasis on individual performance as a criterion of status, which can lead to poor treatment of the less able or less aggressive and an atmosphere of raw competition. What is important, he urges, is that there is opportunity for each person to realize the promise that is in him and to achieve status in terms of his performance with an invitation to excel (24).

Gardner cites two contradictory statements by educators regarding their ideas about individual differences; 1) "I regard it as undemocratic to treat so-called gifted children any differently from other children. To me all children are gifted"; 2) "The goal of the American educational system is to enable every youngster to fulfill his potentialities, regardless of his race, creed social standing or economic position" (87). Gardner says that men are not equal in their native gifts or in their motivations; it follows that they will not be equal in their achievements. This is why equality of opportunity plays such an important role and why we must continually strive to make this a reality, despite great differences that exist such as wealth, learning, concern for education, public vs. private schooling, and wide variations of home and neighborhood environments (14-15). Fortunately, in the U.S., he adds, we recognize that children should have many successive opportunities to discover themselves; and we postpone any final closing of the door on his chances. The late bloomer is not denied his chances at success (81).

ᕱᕲ

Critical Thinking

If a major goal of teaching is to get our students to be substantive thinkers and actors on the real life world stage, then we must give them the tools. Learning how to learn becomes as important as learning about answers. Thus, we must establish patterns of behavior and life skills that students can practice over time and across diverse thinking situations.

Critical thinking involves having the ability to analyze ideas and solve problems, ultimately thinking and acting independently. It includes the ability to take what has already been learned and to synthesize and apply that learning to other topics and real-life situations, in other words, to move beyond basic knowledge, recall, and recitation of facts to higher-level thinking.

Many teachers spend eighty percent of the time asking questions for recall, factual questions that elicit correct answers to specific content. While there are reasons for using these types of questions in order to underscore knowledge or call attention to forgotten ideas, there are higher order levels of questions, which require much more brainpower and more extensive and elaborate answers. One of the most widely applied hierarchies for critical thinking was developed by Benjamin Bloom in his 1956 book, *Taxonomy of Educational Objectives, Handbook I: The Cognitive Domain.* Bloom, who headed a group of educational psychologists, describes learning as having three domains: Cognitive: mental skills (Knowledge and the development of intellectual skills); Affective: growth in feelings or emotional areas (Attitudes); and Psychomotor: manual or physical skills (Skills). In the Cognitive Domain, he identifies six levels of critical thinking, in degree of difficulty; and he challenges educators to progress from asking questions in the "knowledge" category to those that tap higher levels of complex and abstract thinking. I think it useful to note the six question categories as defined by Bloom. (Note: Many use a revised taxonomy, but I prefer the older version.) Bloom and others added active verbs to help educators frame the questions at each level, which I have found to be very effective in my own teaching practice. Several examples of questions are also provided.

Knowledge: recalling data or information: *arrange, define, duplicate, identify, label, list, match, memorize, name, outline, order, recognize, relate, recall, repeat, reproduce, state.*

> ➢ Who, what, when, where, how ….?
> ➢ Describe…

Comprehension: understanding the meaning of information materials and problems as well as describing in one's own words: *classify, comprehend, convert, describe, discuss, distinguish, estimate, explain, express, extend, generalize, infer, interpret, paraphrase, predict, restate (in one's words), review, rewrite, summarize, translate.*

> ➢ Retell…

Application: using previously learned information in new and concrete situations to produce a result or solve a problem:

apply, change, choose, compute, construct, demonstrate, discover, dramatize, illustrate, interpret, manipulate, modify, operate, predict, prepare, produce, relate, show, solve, transfer, use.

➤ How is…an example of…?

➤ How is…related to…?

➤ Why is…significant?

Analysis: separating material or concepts into component parts so that its organizational structure may be understood, making inferences, and/or finding evidence to support generalizations: *analyze, appraise, break down, categorize, compare, contrast, correlate, criticize, differentiate, discriminate, distinguish, examine, experiment, illustrate, infer, outline, question, separate, test.*

➤ What are the parts or features of…?

➤ Classify…according to…

➤ Outline/diagram…

➤ How does…compare/contrast with…?

Synthesis: combining ideas and skills to form a new whole or creating a unique, original product (verbal form or physical object): *adapt, anticipate, collaborate, combine, communicate, compile, compose, create, design, develop, devise, express, facilitate, formulate, generate, hypothesize, incorporate, individualize, initiate, integrate, intervene, invent, model, modify, negotiate, organize, plan, propose, rearrange, reconstruct, reinforce, reorganize, revise, substitute, summarize, validate.*

➤ What would you predict/infer from…?

➤ How would you create/design a new…?

➤ What might happen if you combined…?

➤ What solutions would you suggest for…?

Evaluation: developing opinions, making judgments or decisions about the value of ideas or materials: *appraise, argue,
assess, attach, choose, compare, contrast, conclude, critique,
defend, estimate, evaluate, explain, interpret, judge, justify,
predict, rate, select, support, value.*

> ➤ Do you agree…?
> ➤ What do you think about…?
> ➤ What is the most important…? and why…?
> ➤ What criteria would you use to assess…?

Another way that educators can foster critical thinking for students is
by framing essential questions around big ideas. Grant Wiggins and
Jay McTighe, in *Understanding by Design,* write that big ideas get to
the core of issues, problems, and concepts. In question form, they help
students make sense of important but complicated ideas, knowledge,
and know-how that tend to recur throughout life. Essential questions
lead to genuine inquiry and reflection and invariably proceed to more
questions and new understandings. Students are challenged to consider alternatives, weigh evidence, support their ideas, and justify them.
Through exposure and practice throughout the total school experience,
students learn the skill of rethinking big ideas and assumptions. Their
minds are attuned to continuously make meaningful connections between prior learning and personal experiences (Wiggins and McTighe).

In his book and web site, Wiggins offers many suggestions for making
essential questions that use big ideas. To give an example, a big idea,
which one often frames instinctively as a question or a statement, or
expresses it as a phrase or word, might be "a food chain." An essential
question becomes, "On what energy do we depend and how can we ensure access to it?" I refer you to Wiggins' works for further examination.

Teacher Calvin Roso, in his article "Higher-Level Tweaking," offers
many examples of essential question strategies. He questions state

standards and whether they lead to higher levels of thinking or a tendency to homogenize the curriculum. Roso says, "In part, this depends on the standard; but even more importantly, it depends on what teachers and students do with the standard. We tend to think of aligning our curriculum to set standards, but I believe that part of making the taught curriculum more effective involves teaching our students to think critically."

Roso took a closer look at how he might better align state standards, learning objectives, and student assignments that incorporated higher-level critical thinking skills.

> *"Take an essay test" becomes "Compose an essay differentiating between the issues studied."*
> *"Give a speech" becomes "Analyze issues surrounding the topic of capital punishment, and perform a persuasive speech based on your findings."*
> *"Write a book review" becomes "Critique a book, discussing the author's theme of...."*

I now often tweak state standards by changing the action verbs given in the standard. Bloom's Taxonomy is a great place to get verbiage that will lead students toward higher level/critical thinking skills. For example:

> *"Recognize and explain the impact of ethnic diversity" becomes "Evaluate the impact of ethnic diversity and illustrate a proposal for...."*
> *"Identify and describe the relationship between..." becomes "Interpret the meaning behind each of the...."*

Another method of tweaking aligns standards to multiple intelligences. This not only offers students opportunities to learn in modes that they are strong; it also enables students to develop all of their intelligences to a greater level of competency. To do this, I simply keep a list of learning styles and related activities and revise state standards accordingly:

> *"Recognize and explain the impact of ethnic diversity" becomes "Discuss the impact of ethnic diversity and present a logical proposal for…" or "Dramatize the impact of ethnic diversity and illustrate a proposal for…."*
> *"Identify and describe the relationship between…" becomes "Interpret the meaning behind each of the…, and journal how this relates to your current situation."*
> (Roso)

Visiting schools in different parts of the country, I've observed highly effective practices for students that focus on higher levels of critical thinking. Through professional development, many teachers are becoming more proficient in framing questions around big ideas and incorporating them in their teaching. Whether it takes the form of the *Understanding by Design* model or *Bloom's Taxonomy*'s verbs for formulating questions, educators can place more emphasis on critical thinking in the early grades and increase the sophistication of the questions, activities, and products as students progress.

Other critical thinking strategies include independent study and senior projects, which generally take place at the high school level. A few exceptions have been independent study projects for gifted children at elementary and middle school levels. However, this instructional strategy can work for all students. Independent study has proven effective even at the primary level when it focuses on students' interests or a broad unit of study. What is important is that independent study is guided. Critical thinking, research and study skills are not left to chance. Independent study builds around essential questions that students learn to formulate and likely alter as they pursue their studies. Big questions typically challenge presuppositions and lead to more questions. At the same time, students become more proficient in their research and study skills development. A further skill, which is a natural offshoot, is oral presentation of the project before one's peers. This life skill also needs to be introduced early and practiced.

Critical thinking typically crosses disciplines. Some examples: history can easily pair with visual and performing arts as it is natural to understand the arts and their creators as reflective of the cultures of their times. Scientific discoveries often don't happen in isolation; rather, they are results of past knowledge gained by others' discoveries with social, political, and artistic contexts in play. As educators, we can design more opportunities for rich linkages between our subject areas that connect and create meaningful learning. This requires collaboration of teachers across disciplines. This is challenging, especially for secondary teachers who tend to work more in isolation in their subject departments. It also means more planning time for teachers, preferably built into the schedule. If not allowed during the school day, collaborative planning can be done as a summer professional development project.

The following interdisciplinary and independent study projects are examples of teaching strategies that use higher-level critical and creative thinking. Thomas Rooney, 2004, an English teacher and department chair at Needham High School in Massachusetts, implemented an interdisciplinary *Humanities* course involving English, social studies, and the arts. One of the most popular courses at the school, it not only benefits students, who learn subjects from a very holistic perspective, it facilitates cross-departmental dialogue. Tom also began *Senior Project*, a program where all seniors are required to do a project based on their own interests. Initially, the project began in English classes and then spread to all subject areas. This complex undertaking involves mentorship by a designated teacher and a process of checkpoints monitoring the students' progress. At the end of the year, students present their individual projects to an audience of teachers and students.

Walter Peterson, 1991, an English teacher at Norwood High School in Massachusetts, was recognized for his thirty-one years of outstanding teaching and the successful implementation of a course combining the study of American literature and American history. The principal innovation in the course is the scheduling of major works of literature at the appropriate historical period. Integration of the two disciplines with their concepts and skills becomes very meaningful to student populations that range from underperforming to college prep.

As educators, we can be confident in our abilities to assert what students can and need to learn. Critical thinking skills need to be part of the mix at all levels kindergarten through twelfth grade. I've presented a few of the strategies that educators can use: asking higher thinking questions in our classrooms every day, helping students develop big or essential questions, and collaborating with teachers in other disciplines to develop units of study.

∾

Creativity and Problem Solving

Imagine this scenario: Teenagers from different Eastern European countries, who had at least one year of "book English," are taking classes in English conversation in Poland (I had the wonderful experience of working in four different countries as part of a "Bridges for Education" summer program.). The kids are used to sitting in rows formation and having a teacher stand in front of the class and lecture to them. They then repeat the facts. Oh, what a surprise it was for them to come into a more informal classroom with tables and chairs in a circle, and interact with a teacher who introduced them to brainstorming, discussing some big questions that encouraged them to think critically about issues in their own lives, and accomplishing some independent study projects of their choice. It was truly amazing to see their progress in three weeks time both in fluency of conversation and ideas and critical and creative thinking. In the beginning, students were uncomfortable; it took several tries to introduce these new learning skills. But rising to the challenge, they became rather delighted in themselves and were full of enthusiasm and motivation as they practiced their new-found abilities.

Ahas come in all voltages. Oh, the wonder of seeing the light in a student's eyes as she comes up with an insight, solution to a problem, or new expression. Considering much of the research on creativity and having worked with students and teachers at all levels, I am convinced we all have capacity to be creative, and we all create in different and valuable ways. Creativity can be fostered, and we can all grow in creative behavior. Latent in all of us, creativity just needs opportunities to surface. This has implication for educators about how we establish a climate conducive to encouraging creativity and the types of questions and strategies that we incorporate in our teaching. We can stimulate creativity by having our students examine what is, explore what might be, and evaluate. The more we observe, the more we attend to with all of our senses and the more raw material we have for making mental connections that result in new and relevant ideas. As educators, we can provide as much fuel as possible to feed the brain from a variety of sources in order to enable rich associations. We can practice problem solving and creative thinking with our students so that these skills become internalized. We can remove the brakes that we put on imaginations and set up discussions and experiences that put pre-judgments aside. A most powerful way to develop creativity in your students is to be a role model, which means clarifying your own values, goals, and ideas about creativity and showing them in your actions. The teachers you likely remember are those whose thoughts and actions served as your role models, who balanced content with teaching you how to think about that content.

Creativity has been studied from many perspectives, including but not limited to: behavioral psychology, social psychology, education, cognitive science, philosophy, history, economics, design research, business, and art. While there is no single, authoritative perspective or definition of creativity, several underlying concepts emerge. 1) Creativity is a mental process involving the generation of new ideas, insights or concepts, novel approaches, or new associations between existing ideas or concepts. 2) Creativity is the act of making something new that is original and appropriate. The products of creative thought include some obvious things like music, poetry, dance, drama, literature, inventions, and technical innovations. But there are some less obvious examples as well, such as envisioning many possible solutions, challenging presuppositions, or seeing the world in imaginative and different ways.

Much of the work on creativity stemmed from initial research on the nature of intelligence, which led to study of education of gifted and talented youth. While still advocating for attention to the needs of and differentiated education for gifted and talented students, I believe that many instructional strategies developed for them can be used in traditional classrooms for all students. A review of the literature leads me to a synthesis of the ideas and strategies for teaching creativity from a number of notable educators, and I encourage further reading of their studies and application of their ideas: E. Paul Torrance, who developed the Torrance Tests of Creative Thinking, which showed that the IQ test was not the only way to measure intelligence; Joseph Renzulli; Donald Treffinger; Sidney Parnes; Robert Sternberg and Wendy M. Williams at the Center for Development and Learning in Covington LA; George Prince of Synectics, an engineering firm that taught adults and students creative problem solving; Peter Facione at Santa Clara University, CA; and educators at The International Center for Studies in Creativity at Buffalo State University of New York.

How can you be more creative, and help your students be more creative? The International Center for Studies in Creativity at Buffalo State University of New York says, "Creativity is an effective resource that resides in all people and within all organizations. Our more than thirty years of research has conclusively demonstrated that creativity can be nurtured and enhanced through the use of deliberate tools, techniques, and strategies through which students can develop essential life skills that they can apply to their lives" (Center for Studies in Creativity).

The following instructional approaches have proven to be helpful when practiced over time, not taught in isolation but incorporated within units of instruction.

Establish a creative environment.
Might one establish a school environment that moves beyond routine thinking to speculative thinking? It certainly would get beyond answers that are black or white and seeing things on very concrete levels

to situations, where there are lots of ideas that are exciting, confusing, ambiguous, and seemingly disconnected—a kind of intellectual playfulness. It's more process than product oriented, and it encourages kids to take risks without fear of self-censoring and worrying whether their ideas are dumb or good or bad. Making mistakes is OK; in fact, when students make mistakes it's a perfect opportunity to get them to analyze and discuss them. Often these errors contain the germ of correct answers or good ideas.

Our classrooms can be places that encourage and reward initiative, inquisitiveness, and originality. A climate that fosters openness is one in which there is a free flow exchange of ideas, where assumptions can be challenged, and ambiguity is allowed. Questioning is encouraged, and students are guided to ask the kind of thoughtful questions that require answers that go beyond recitation of facts.

<u>Focus on divergent thinking skills.</u>
Most researchers agree that the following concepts apply to activities that encourage creative thinking:

> ➢ Generate ideas for any given situation, both in number (fluency) and in-kind (flexibility). The more ideas generated, the larger the base for finding the best solution.
> ➢ Solicit free thinking of unusual ideas, bizarre notions, and even outlandish scenarios. An implausible idea may spark a workable one or one that can be modified to fit a solution or strategy.
> ➢ Defer judgment during idea generation or problem solving as it becomes inhibiting to students and the process itself.
> ➢ Combine ideas. It's not unusual for one idea to spawn another, which often becomes apparent in group work. By joining unlikely ideas, new and original solutions arise.

Brainstorming or generating ideas and alternatives to a situation is an effective divergent thinking teaching strategy. Some examples of teachers' questions are:

> List as many…as you can think of.
> What would happen if…were true?
> Suppose you could have…. How would you use it?
> How would this look to a…?
> How would you feel if you were…?
> How is…like…?

<u>Encourage complex thinking and feeling processes.</u>

How to manage conflicting ideas, how to juggle possibilities; these are skills that adults as well as children need. In addition to providing an atmosphere that encourages numerous new ideas, possibilities, and alternatives, teachers can use many methods, both cognitive and affective, that get students to utilize ideas in complex situations that deal with complex feelings, tensions, and conflict. These involve the use of higher level thinking skills that go beyond fact acquisition and recall and encourage students to "apply, analyze, synthesize, and evaluate" their ideas and work (Bloom's Taxonomy). Role playing, simulations, problem solving, research skills, and values clarification are some effective techniques for students to apply their knowledge and skills as they develop their projects (elaboration), finalize and authenticate their work (expression), and then verify it to its effectiveness (evaluation).

<u>Foster independence.</u>

Donald Treffinger adds that reaching independence, the level in which students learn to manage and direct their own behaviors for inquiry and learning, managing resources, and creatively solving problems, is a major goal. Like other learning skills, students need experiences in 1) functioning more effectively in one's total environment (classroom, school, home, and community) with peers, teachers, parent, and other adults; 2) making choices and decisions based on self-knowledge of their needs and interests; 3) assuming responsibility for completion of these activities at a satisfactory level of achievement and an acceptable time frame; 4) learning to define problems and determine a course of action; and 5) evaluating one's own work. In the affective domain, Treffinger cites Maslow, who describes the progression toward self-actualization, internalization of values, and commitment to a creative, productive lifestyle (Treffinger).

Allow time for incubation of ideas and responses.

Our lives are fast paced, and often we value quickness of response in all forms. However, most effective results don't happen quickly. We all need time to understand a problem and toss it around. We need time that is open and flexible for unpredicted developments to happen during exploration or ideas to pop up while we are relaxing or doing other things. We need time to allow ideas to converge and perhaps come up with better ones. If tests, assignments, and activities are packed with instant response formats, then we're not giving students time to be thoughtful and express themselves in ways that represent a synthesis between their thoughts and those of others.

Integrate problem solving activities, big and small.

Learning by discovery and involvement in real challenges requires a teaching-learning strategy that sets conditions to make discovery possible. The process of inquiry or inductive sequence starts when the learner is confronted with problem situations that create a feeling of bafflement. Then the student can analyze, manipulate and experiment, either symbolically or actually, to transform the information and reassemble it to get new insights (Taba 350-352). One can build learning experiences around children's natural curiosity by dealing with problems relevant to their own needs, purposes, and interests. I'm reminded of the elementary student council that responded to needs in their school as well as those of the broader community (see "Torches: Leadership"). Real life experiences that call for active participation in problem solving is another avenue, and most academic subjects lend themselves to hands-on problem solving activities. It might not be as elaborate as the CSI model used by Lanie Higgins in her classroom (see "Rays of Sunshine: A Time of Wonder"); yet there are so many instances in science or math, for example, where students can test water quality in their environments or compute expenses of their households. Educators can further stimulate creativity by helping students to think across subjects and disciplines. Learning in most schools often occurs in discrete boxes—the math box, the social studies box, the science box, while cross-fertilization can draw on students' interests and abilities (Sternberg).

The collaborative group experience is another example of a life skill that is important for students to learn, for it is this process in which students learn to imagine other viewpoints, learn by example, and practice working with others. "That person knows things I don't, and so in those areas I can learn from him. I know things that he or she does not, so he/she can learn from me in those areas. Neither of us has any right to punish the other. We avoid entering into win/lose discussions, although we are available to discuss and resolve differences. We don't have to be one-up or one-down" (Prince).

Who could have imagined some of this generation's complex issues of climate change, inequality of opportunity, competition vs. cooperation in addressing international needs of scarce resources, terrorism, and proliferation of weaponry? It's important to recognize that students in our schools today may confront entirely new problems when they are adults, many which we can't anticipate. Students need the tools to deal with problems effectively and creatively on their own, in effect having life skills for dealing with their futures.

Model creativity

A most powerful way to develop creativity in your students is to be a role model, which means clarifying your own values, goals, and ideas about creativity and showing them in your actions. Understanding that children learn in different ways, alternative learning strategies can be provided. This involves being creative in putting kids in touch with books, people, labs, experiences, and resources of all kinds, which stimulate their curiosity and feed their interests. Activities and units can be flexible enough to encourage exploration and invention. It's about providing challenge rather than pressure. And it's being a resource and facilitator of learning rather than a dispenser of information. As in other areas of excellence that have been explored, approaches for fostering creativity need practice over the span of time, not taught as solo teaching strategies but incorporated within units of instruction.

To summarize, many ideas and techniques have been published and practiced in both education and industry to enhance creative thinking abilities. Rather than becoming lessons by themselves, they can be integrated effectively with content in any subject, discipline, or student interest.

ᐤᧈ

Study Skills

We want our students to become independent thinkers and practitioners. They will not come by this goal easily; instead, they will need guidance and practice over time. The process involves learning persistence and getting it right by hard work. It's an antidote to the immediate gratification kids want and experience in all phases of their lives. Using effective study skills has implications for the future and how students deal with organization and management of time, materials, and selves in any post secondary school or work setting. (Sizer T. 38)

Homework can be justified if it's dutiful. Students need to practice what they're learning; often, there just isn't sufficient class time to do this. Ted Sizer in *Keeping Schools: Letters to Families* writes a letter to parents. "Homework is a means not an end. For me simply to assign 'the first two chapters' unintentionally missed the point. Better that I had told my class that tomorrow we would discuss the introduction of one of the key characters in the novel and that I would query each student on some aspect of the author's introductions of this dramatis persona. (I would even expect them to know what dramatis persona meant)" (38). Teachers can encourage parents to arrange a designated time and place in the home, which helps foster good study habits. A table in a well-lit area works just fine. Quiet helps, too. The student and others in the family need to know that this study time is part of the "contract" between home and school, which needs to be fully respected.

By setting clear expectations both orally and in writing, educators can help students with different learning styles to understand assignments. Parents, too, need to go beyond assumptions that their children intuitively know what they're thinking or saying. And being consistent in how and when all guardians at home and school deal with most matters is also important. Kids like boundaries even though they'll do everything possible to wiggle out of them. This, however, doesn't mean total inflexibility.

"SQ3R." Survey! Question! Read! Recite! Review! I remember when this formula was introduced in the 1960s as the teaching of study skills accompanied the teaching of reading—and there seems to have been a different formula each decade since. SQ3R provided a framework for the reader to get set for the task of reading. I liken it to preparation one takes before painting a wall—sanding, cleaning, and painting test and primary coats. Study skills, which give students a context and purpose for learning, prove to be helpful in various learning situations: reading of a chapter, response to a test question, and prelude to a written composition or an oral presentation. I've used the concept with college as well as K-12 students and think it worthwhile to recapitulate. For example, consider a homework assignment to read several chapters in a social studies book where students apply the steps.

<u>Survey</u> gathers information necessary to focus and formulate goals. Quickly, students preview the book's table of contents and see where the chapters fit with the whole scheme of the topic or unit. They take a few minutes to look at the title, headings, and subheadings (usually in bold), captions and pictures, charts and graphs. They then survey

the introductory and concluding paragraphs and any review questions or study guide.

Question helps the mind engage and concentrate by searching for answers. While surveying, students turn the title, headings and subheadings into questions. They ask themselves, "What do I already know about this chapter, and what did my teacher say about this chapter when it was assigned?"

Read fills in information around the previewing and questioning. As they read, students reread captions and note all underlined, italicized, bold printed words. They reduce speed for difficult passages and reread parts that aren't clear. Then they read a section at a time and recite after each section.

Recite helps the mind to concentrate and learn as it reads. Students use a form of recitation that best suits their learning styles. They can underline, highlight important points, or take notes from the text but write them in their own words. Finally, they orally summarize what they've just read. It has been found that the more senses one uses, the better the memory.

Review is an ongoing process. It can include: paging through the text and notebook to review important points, writing questions in the margins that are highlighted or underlined, making flash cards for those questions that present difficulty, or developing mnemonic devices for material which needs to be memorized (Robinson).

⁓

Mentoring

"I feel lost," explains a Vietnamese American teenager when interviewed by Maria Cramer for her article, "Disconnected," published in the *Boston Globe* on May 27, 2008. This teen is not alone. Many kids can't talk to parents about their emotional problems even when they are unbearable. Parents struggle with jobs requiring long hours and low wages, and often they are just too busy to talk with their kids. Typically, among many new immigrant groups, their primary focus is to get their children to succeed in ways they couldn't. Parents tell their kids to get good grades and go to college, but they don't have time to talk about what's happening in their lives. According to Cramer, surveys of schoolchildren, including those who are truant, involved with gangs, or have been arrested, indicate a major need—"We need adults who can encourage us" (B1-6).

There are so many issues confronting high school children today: risk of failure, lack of motivation, family problems, peer pressure, and over-prioritizing. I've had opportunities to visit several high school classes that happened to be presenting what they viewed as their personal issues in a fast changing world. Chief among their concerns is anonymity. "Who am I? Where am I going? How do I get there? What's the purpose?" They expressed their solutions, which I endorse. They want a voice in problem solving and encourage venues for doing this with teachers and administrators. They do better in smaller classes. They want to have proactive group discussions on matters such as nutrition, anorexia/bulimia, and cutting. They need support in learning how to prioritize among their many school and life choices.

All kids need role models. I am not suggesting that educators take on the role of parents, but that they should be mindful of their students' total life experiences both in and out of school. Whenever possible, they can reach out to kids and really get to know them. Here are a few possible strategies. A number of schools at all levels, K-12, designate teachers to one or more students each in order to really listen to what's on their minds and ask questions that get them thinking about choices or solving problems. This is not a fleeting experience of one or two meetings. It's an enduring relationship. This way kids feel that there is someone with whom to check in or to discuss an issue. Bill Horewitch, the physical ed coach who is profiled in "Spotlights: The Whole Child," set up one such primary school mentoring program in rural Texas that serves underprivileged children. Other teacher/student pairing programs at the secondary level serve as models that often proactively deal with problems before they come to the reactive attention of a guidance counselor or administrator. In addition, there are educators who coordinate enrichment activities after school or show up at some extracurricular activities like plays, concerts, and sporting events to show their support for students.

I think it is also important for educators to share with their students what they do outside of school: their interests, hobbies, travel, and professional development activities. This provides further confirmation of personal commitment to lifelong learning, models its importance, and conveys the sheer enjoyment of adding to one's experiences. I'm reminded of "The Hero Project," integrated with an English course at Framingham High School in Massachusetts where Marc Banks, 2008, has each student tackling a brand new skill of choice: keeping a journal of discoveries, mishaps, and new directions; and making a final presentation to the class. Marc sets an example by going through the same experience at the same time and sharing his own Hero Project.

Many of us have been touched by a teacher or some one person in the community or workplace who was in a teaching or mentor role, who really saw us, listened to what we said or did not say, and encouraged and inspired us to be "all that we can be." Young or old, individuals know the importance and long-term impact of a good teacher, role model, and mentor in their lives. One year an unusual number of student nominators took the time to reflect on their current and former teachers. Their comments do more justice to the theme of mentoring than what I could elaborate. Here are a few excerpts that convey how excellent educators can truly make a difference:

> *I first met Mrs. T back in 1988 when she was my kindergarten teacher. She taught me not only the basics of writing, math, and reading but much more. She also taught me about teamwork and social and people skills.* (This student has been coming back as a teacher's aide to Mrs. T while in middle school and high school.)

> An eighth grader writes, *"I want to nominate Mr. P. because he has been a positive role model for me and for my fellow peers. He has shown that you are never too young to make a difference in others' lives. He is able to talk to me and my peers as if we are real people, and not kids who have to have all the knowledge that he has to offer crammed into their minds. We are able to learn how to live life to the fullest from our experiences."*

> *Mrs. E and I teach math together. I don't know how I would have made it through the past three and a half years without her help. A new teacher is at high risk, and success can only be accomplished with strong support. Mrs. E. explained our lessons during our weekly meetings, allowed me to observe her classes, and coached me on managing all of the responsibilities that come with being a teacher.*

> *Mr. T. has been my seventh and eighth grade English teacher. He has a certain magical quality that enables him to turn an average child into an exceptional one, a certain quality that makes children want to learn more and not be ashamed to ask why.*

A high school graduate notes, *"Mr. H is the only real adult mentor in my life. Never have I met another adult who so easily connects with his younger students and is so influential in their lives. Even after I left elementary school, he remained a true mentor. He made an appearance at one of my high school basketball games and even one of my soccer games. He continued to invite us girls to come back and work on our jump shots whenever we felt rusty. He always checked in on our grades and asked us how our classes were going. I even got a phone call from him during the stressful time of college decision-making. He asked me about the colleges I was considering, gave me his two cents, and assured me that I would make the right decision."* Another student also comments about Mr. H., *"I am very thankful to have someone like him in my life. He is much more that a coach or teacher to me. He is family and I love him."*

I have had the privilege of seeing two different sides of Mrs. M. I have been her student. I am now her colleague. She is the reason I became an English teacher. In junior high, she cared about every student in the class. She cared about what we learned. She cared about how we learned. She cared about our success as students and as people. Her love of teaching and kids shone through every day. As I continue in my eleventh year as an English teacher, I strive to emulate Mrs. M.

☙

Professional Development

"Ongoing learning and training for faculty and staff are essential for schools as they move away from teaching students how to succeed in a 20th century manufacturing economy to teaching them how to excel in today's 21st century technology age" (Houston A+ Challenge). Sometimes it means revisiting themes and ideas that come back for another cycle, like strategies for teaching "New Math." At other times it involves exploring new concepts and technologies that been developed in response to our changing times. New teachers need information about practical practices and strategies that weren't fully addressed in their teacher prep classes at college; veteran teachers require updates and continued coaching; administrators need collegial support systems.

There is increasing recognition that teachers should be at the center of reform efforts and have control over their own professional learning needs; there are many ways to accomplish this. One effective practice is the *Critical Friends Group* (CFG) developed by the Annenberg Institute for School Reform in 1994, which has been implemented in many schools throughout the U.S. Participants draw on each other's skills and ideas, as well as knowledge bases outside the school, to design a program and expand their repertoires of teaching in their own environments. Collaboratively, Critical Friends Group members establish student learning goals, help each other think about better teaching practices, look closely at curriculum and student work, and identify school culture issues that affect student achievement. A CFG professional learning community typically consists of approximately eight to twelve educators who come together voluntarily at least once a month for about two hours. The group has a coach who facilitates a protocol for examining students' work brought in my members. CFG coaches are trained to create a collegial culture within the group and use a number of vehicles to engage their colleagues: examining student and teacher work, solving problems, discussing texts, observing peers, setting goals, building teams, and creating teacher portfolios.

The CFG concept appears to work really well, especially when a principal publicly supports the CFG group. This may include providing time during the school day and providing substitute teachers to cover classrooms when CFG teachers are participating in peer observations (Houston A+ Challenge; Dunne, Nave, and Lewis 9-12).

Professional development can be valued as an on-going nurturing process for all teachers, new and veteran, in a school and district. Opportunities and resources can be provided by the building principal based upon specific needs and wants. The district, too, can encourage support that goes across grade levels. Vertical team meetings is an example of constructive dialog that occurs among representatives of different grade levels who meet to discuss scope and sequence for the purpose of facilitating curriculum continuity and eliminating repetition. "Vertical teaming" or "curriculum spiraling" between elementary and secondary level teachers offers insight as to "who's doing what and when" and establishes a logical sequence of content and skills. Methodology also comes into play. I remember a time when there was much discussion of how best to teach a large block of ninety minutes at the high school in contrast to the usual forty-minute period, when it was decided to provide a greater amount of time for in-depth study of major subjects. Many high school teachers were at first uncomfortable with the new instructional block. So, who became the resources? None other than elementary teachers, who were used to the concept and became invaluable with their suggestions.

Educators often view remuneration for specific work such as summer curriculum development or paying for conferences and substitutes as recognition for their efforts. It's one thing to encourage professional development; providing additional pay and/or credits toward certification or graduate degrees validate the process. Capitalizing on the talents of excellent teachers utilizing a train-the-trainer approach or "Teacher Leaders" described in the "Reflections: Leadership" chapter is another model.

There are several programs that aren't based on the typical professional development format. One encourages teachers to take courses of their choice at local colleges, either as enrichment such as a literature course or exposure to other content areas. Some colleges in New England, for example, have collaborated with local school districts to offer this program. There are dividends. Teachers from different districts participate and use the opportunity to share ideas. Another professional development format is the "job-alike" concept that encourages people from different school districts to convene at regular meetings to address issues of common concern, discuss strategies that work and don't work, and "show and tell." I facilitated many "job alike" groups hosted by a regional collaborative, which held monthly meetings of people from different school systems with similar responsibilities such as Social Studies Directors, Assistant Superintendents for Curriculum and Instruction, and Foreign Language Directors (as many as fifteen different groups and counting), who met for years to discuss and advise on issues facing all of them. They developed regional professional development programs that met their needs; they counted on each other's support, and they continually learned from one another. The job-alike concept provided a wonderful vehicle for cross-fertilization of ideas and practices.

Recognizing that there is always more and more information to distill and digest, educators know the importance of lifelong learning as integral to their profession. Their commitment pays off and provides a model for their students. I've often thought that if I take a nugget or two from each of the professional development experiences that I've had, I'm way ahead.

ॐ

Teacher Retention

"Here they come, and I'm not ready. How could I be? I'm a new teacher and learning on the job." Musing on his first days in the classroom in the McKee Vocational and Technical HD in Staten Island, New York, Frank McCourt writes, "Professors of Education at NYU never lectured about how to handle flying sandwich situations. They talked about the theories and philosophies of education, about moral and ethical imperatives, about the necessity of dealing with the whole child, the child's needs, but never about critical moments in the classroom" (19). McCourt remembered a professor, who coached that "before your students enter a room, you must decide your posture and placement. You stand in the hallway to face the swarm, you never let them invade your territory, and never sit or even stand behind your desk. And I thought teaching was a simple matter of telling the class what you knew and then testing them and giving them grades" (40). After eight years at the inner city school, he states, "I still struggled to hold the attention of five classes every day though I was learning what was obvious. You have to make your own way in the classroom. You have to find yourself. You have to develop your own style, your own techniques. You have to tell the truth or you'll be found out... 'Oh, teacher man, that's not what you said last week'" (113). McCourt learned his craft by trial and error, that there is much more than keeping students quiet and in their seats. His methods weren't conventional, yet by his force of nature, he created a lasting impact on his students. He reached students through the backdoor of imagination with storytelling, assignments like creating an "absent note" from Adam/Eve to God, sing-alongs to remember concepts, and field trips such as taking twenty-nine rowdy girls to a movie in Times Square and later to see Shakespeare's *Hamlet*.

McCourt could have profited from an early mentoring program; he might have received more supervision and guidance; he might have had opportunities to observe veteran teachers. Somehow, he stayed unlike others who choose to leave the profession. In fact, retaining quality teachers is an on-going challenge. Nationally, one-third of teachers leave within three years, one-half leaves within five years, and the percentage is higher in urban settings. Much research on the issue shows that wages are a driving force; teacher training programs need improvement; classroom size is often too large; teachers need more support for their own social emotional issues as they cope with the initial survival stage of teaching; and high stakes testing puts much pressure on teachers.

A number of initiatives tackle the problem. The DuBarry Open Circle Teacher Retention Initiative explores and capitalizes on the links between social and emotional learning, reflective practice, and the success and retention of new teachers. Their research evidences classroom management is the most common problem area reported by new teachers and principals. In addition, new teachers are unable to deal with uncertainly and behavior that is unexplained, and they lack cultural awareness to teach to culturally and racially diverse students. The initiative encourages professional development as early as the first year to address these issues. It endorses relationships with other adults in the school setting including veteran teachers, like-minded peers, administrators, and formal mentors. The process of starting a teaching career doesn't have to be perceived as a lone venture, but rather one that is braced by the companionship, empathy, and wisdom of coworkers (Murray and Vetter).

Many school districts face the challenge of replacing experienced staff with those who are less experienced. One way to ensure quality and excellence during the transition is to use the expertise of experienced teachers by offering mentor programs. Some states have legislated this process while others leave it to individual schools districts to implement. There are many models. One that has impressed me is Dover-Sherborn's in suburban Boston, which has formalized a mentor program for the entire system. Each new teacher is assigned a mentor, who receives additional support from the principal, teacher leader, department head, and other appropriate staff members. The new teacher has the responsibility to seek help, be forthright in communicating classroom problems, be open to feedback, and make structured observations of her mentors and other veteran teachers. The key to the program is the team of teacher leaders, who designed the program. Their charge is to coordinate the program among different school buildings, oversee it, and train the mentors. This latter step is highly important, as the skill of mentoring is not taken for granted. The teacher leaders also hold afternoon workshops for new teachers and their mentors, and they organize observation days for them. Teacher leaders get a stipend as well as professional development credit (Dover-Sherborn Mentor Program 19-20).

Goldin Foundation Educators of Excellence recommend careful matching of mentors. They emphasize the importance of finding the right person with whom to interact on a regular basis. Often the decision for matching is made by the building principal, which doesn't quite fit the bill. For the new teacher, this suggests more direct involvement in finding a mentor should an assigned one not meet his/her needs. It might necessitate seeking a teacher with whom he has made a connection in order to establish another, but less formal mentorship.

The issues of testing and accountability also have implication for teacher retention, especially when there is huge pressure to raise achievement, competition among schools and teachers, and disagreement about salaries. While educators recognize the value of standardized tests as tools for assessing strengths and weaknesses of districts and individual children, they express several concerns. Should monetary rewards be given to schools, districts, and teachers whose students do well? To whom should monies be awarded–math, science, and engineering teachers? What about teachers in other subject areas or those who mentor or assume leadership roles? Are we emphasizing too much time on test preparation in order to meet standards? Many teachers seem overwhelmed by the enormous amount of time spent on practicing strategies for answering short answer questions, reading short paragraphs, and filling in spaces for the correct answers. They express dissatisfaction that there is less time for teaching skills involving longer assignments that require students to read, write, handle different points of view, and solve real problems. Are standardized tests designed to measure facts? An informal consensus concludes that they do not measure higher-level critical thinking skills, problem solving ability, creativity, and persistence.

The reform/accountability/standards orientation is at times in conflict with teacher autonomy. In her article, "Why Teachers Quit," Kimberly Palmer describes the experience of a teacher. "It wasn't her teenage students who drove her out of teaching—it was the crippling inflexibility of her administrators. All the innovative curriculum ideas and field trips she proposed to engage her tenth grade biology students were promptly shot down, and she left the profession after just two years." Despite her enjoyment of teaching, she couldn't handle the bureaucracy and reform pressures. A report on teacher attrition by the federal National Center for Education Statistics notes comments from former teachers, who took non-education jobs, that they had less professional autonomy and less influence over policies at school than in their current jobs (Palmer 45).

It's interesting that there are contradictory opinions about percentages of teachers leaving the profession. An article "Teachers Tell Researchers They Like Their Jobs," by Vaishali Honawar, reported that 93 percent of teachers were satisfied with their jobs after entering their field, attrition rates being actually lower than for other professionals. The same National Center for Education Statistics surveyed nine thousand graduates (1992-93), who received their bachelor degrees in various disciplines, with 20 percent of those entering the teaching profession. Their findings showed that teacher turnover rates are actually lower than those in other professions and are part of the normal sorting process (Honawar).

What is clear is the U.S. faces a shortage of teaching talent, as 2.8 million teachers need to be recruited over the next eight years due to baby-boomer retirement, increasing student enrollment and staff turnover. We need to find and keep high quality teachers. "Research suggests that a good teacher is the single most important factor in boosting achievement, more important that class size, the dollars spent per student, or the quality of books and materials" (Wallis 13). Many experiments attract, reward, and retain teachers. Some include ideas borrowed from business: signing bonuses, extra pay for teaching in distressed schools, merit pay based on the quality of teacher performance, and bonuses based on raising test scores. These solutions are debatable (Wallis 15).

There is no one magic formula for teacher retention. I think various groups are responsible and can act decisively, individually, and in co-operation with each other. To posit a possible scenario:

> ➢ Colleges and universities prepare students to have deep knowledge of their subjects, which is especially important for teaching at secondary levels.
> ➢ At teacher training institutions, instructors who have direct experience in classrooms provide teaching strategies and on-going supervision during student teaching. Their responsibility is twofold, not only attract, but also ensure the best possible candidates who will work with children. This may necessitate discouraging some people for whom the profession is not a good fit.
> ➢ School districts provide mentoring and professional development opportunities; and they develop budgets that keep student loads to levels where there's room for some personalization.
> ➢ Building administrators encourage teacher autonomy, value their input in decision making including how their work is judged, and build on the strengths of individuals and partners in the community.

> ➤ Collegial groups of educators provide on-going reflection and support of each other using common planning time by grade levels and across grades by subject areas.
> ➤ Teachers have roles in defining their needs and interests.
> ➤ In recognition for time spent mentoring or taking leadership roles, teachers are awarded professional development credits towards recertification or receive stipends.

Developing a twenty-first century educational system needs to be a priority, and it will take a collective responsibility to make it one of quality. The nation at large needs a coherent and inspirational group of people to help change the paradigm and recognize the vital role of educators. Both federal and state governments need to be involved. There is need for consistency of task and message; school districts should not be spending valued time annually considering how they will cut services and having programs that are on-again, off- again. It may be time for a national dialogue. Perhaps we need to rethink the formulas for funding schools; maybe we can consider teacher unions, institutions of higher learning, and community groups as partners, not antagonists. We all need to listen more fully.

I am heartened there are excellent committed people across the country who have chosen to teach our children. These teachers do everything in their power to maximize students' potential! Many enter the profession directly from college; some are inspired to serve in inner city schools under the auspices of organizations like Teach for America; others enter the profession later as they choose to change careers. There are veteran teachers taking on the challenge of being teacher leaders, who mentor student teachers and interns and new teachers in their buildings, as well as many retired teachers and administrators, who continue to serve in some ways. These educators are willing and able and excited to be part of the great experience of making a difference in children's lives. They need to be valued, recognized, and rewarded.

ᗧᖱ

Early Childhood Education

We have to start educating children earlier in the U.S. in order to diminish the inequality of opportunities: family structure, socioeconomic status, non-English speaking, and racial barriers. My experiences in visiting schools in different states, participating in early efforts at pairing schools with universities to foster desegregation, and speaking with numerous administrators lead to my conclusion that a concerted effort for early childhood education is imperative. Of the many school reforms to tackle, universal preschool education could propel us in the right direction for the future. The choices of implementation can vary, but quality of programming must be assured. Whether it's Head Start or nursery school, there is no better option for our society than providing opportunities for getting all kids better prepared to learn. The benefits are many: reduction of underachieving and unmotivated students, increased academic performance throughout the grade levels, less need for remediation, decreased school failure, reduced drop-out rate for high school students, with its corollary of increased high school graduation, and potentially increased college attendance.

I've sometimes thought that school systems should "require" or better yet, "strongly suggest" courses for parents when their students are enrolled in kindergarten and pre-kindergarten. A host of issues needs to be addressed, and we may be making assumptions about what parents know. Does the unmarried teenager with kids or even the supercharged professional mom and/or dad know how to better partner with their schools? Do they know what the expectations are, or how to deal with common issues such as homework, bullying, and setting clear boundaries for their children? Just consider one topic among hundreds that could serve as a point of discussion. Lynne Reeves Griffin in *Negotiation Generation: Take Back Your Parental Authority without Punishment,* writes, "We might take a few cues from proactive parenting." She notes the reality of two income families, juggling childcare, and increasing hectic schedules. Feeling a little guilty and trying to enjoy the little time they have with their kids, they often let bad behavior slide, treat kids like pals, or shower them with gifts. She suggests that children who don't listen have parents who talk too much. Today's parents, who are the "negotiation generation," would be better off setting clear, consistent boundaries. Once the rules are in place, they're non-negotiable. Discussing them is pointless and counterproductive. That doesn't mean that parents can't offer age appropriate choices as a way of "granting freedoms within the fences" (Griffin).

My feeling is that schools should continue proactive parenting education throughout the continuum of a child's education. There's got to be more than the one night visit a year to "Open House" at the middle or high school. School administrators, in tandem with parent groups, can offer sessions on timely topics and encourage teachers in the building to also attend.

I agree with many of the recommendations of the National Education Association, which advocates for universal preschool education among other strategies to close the achievement gap. The report states that while there have been successes, a brief look at the results of the 2002 federal act, "No Child Left Behind" evidences a huge increase in dropout rates, especially for disadvantaged students. "While some students are improving, clear achievement gaps exist within school systems. There are strategies to close such gaps, strategies that move beyond simply training students for test taking." While they likely would require an increase in spending for public schools, these reforms emphasize personal attention for students, parents, and educators:

- ➤ Consider students' diversities and assets to increase teachers' cultural competence.
- ➤ Screen children early for medical or social services, and identify students who need additional instructional support.
- ➤ Engage and reach out to students' families by establishing family centers at schools and other community locations, hiring staff from the community who speak families' home languages, pro-

viding transportation to and from school events, and conducting adult education and parenting courses at local schools.

➢ Institute full day kindergarten and pre-kindergarten.

➢ Reorganize the instructional day to maximize time for learning.

➢ Extend learning to before- and after-school programs as well as summer programs.

➢ Improve teacher education programs. Recruit, develop, and retain qualified teachers and para-educators.

➢ Provide time for faculty to meet and plan, and compensate those teachers who take on extra responsibilities.

➢ Provide additional resources and support for students experiencing achievement gaps.

➢ Engage teachers in strengthening curriculum and student assessments.

➢ Decrease class size.

(Data compiled from *The Boston Globe*, Mass Advocates for Children, *Children's Data Bank*, National Center for Education Statistics, National Education Association, and Boston Partners in Education.)

A recent study conducted in the United Kingdom showed that children who went to preschool perform better in math at age ten than their classmates who didn't get early education, scoring twenty-seven percent higher on a standard test. By attending preschool for eighteen months on average, children's cognitive language and social development were boosted, and they were more ready to benefit from the elementary school experience. "The finding may buttress the case made by advocates of universal preschool education in the U.S., where the federal government provides such programs only for children from low-income families. By contrast the UK has paid for preschool for all three and four year olds since 2004, regardless of their parents' earnings" (Ostrow A2).

I'm encouraged by some state initiatives that have committed to building universal pre-school programs. "A study by Georgetown University released in June, 2008, found that students who had completed

Tulsa, Oklahoma's state-funded program exceeded peers, who did not attend, in reading, writing, and math. Oklahoma is one of only three states that fund public preschool education" (Ostrow A2). Some pilot programs in Massachusetts and North Carolina noted that after receiving grants, they were able to provide a longer preschool day, which was a boon for working parents; more money for teachers who were working longer days; and reduced staff turnover (Ostrow A2). Providing universal preschool in the U.S. means investing in an infrastructure that involves more than the opening of schools. Children are likely to get the most benefit when there is accreditation, college educated teachers, and parents who are actively engaged.

In addition to advocacy for early childhood programs, there is a growing movement that urges other family and community programs to be part of the paradigm shift for change in children's achievement. Paul Tough reviews Susan Neuman's book, *Changing the Odds for Children at Risk*, which describes non-school intervention programs that work: Nurse-Family Partnerships, which sends trained nurses to visit and counsel poor mothers during and after their pregnancies; Early Head Start, a federal program that offers low-income families parental support, medical care, and daycare centers during the first three years of children's lives; and a language enrichment program for Spanish speaking parents (Tough 17-19).

If I could act on my thoughts, I would incorporate universal healthcare in the mix because children need to be able to thrive physically along with cognitive development. If we are to move education forward with implications for the well being and growth of our society in this new century, we must work to educate the whole child from the time they start learning before kindergarten through grade 12 and higher education. We can reinforce motivation. We can increase achievement. We can encourage lifelong learning.

༄

Civic Education

"Participatory democracy," according to John Dewey, emphasizes that "democracy is much more than a form of government. It is a way of life in which all citizens actively, and appropriately, participate in making and implementing all the communal, societal, and institutional decisions that significantly shape their lives" (Benson, Harkavy, and Puckett 131). In *Dewey's Dream*, the latter remind us of John Dewey's crusade for participatory democracy in the late 1800s. As factories replaced households as centers of production, work became separate and distant from home and neighborhood. Children had less opportunity to mix with adults other than their teachers and parents, who became busier. Dewey posited that in industrial societies, formal schooling and learning must replace the informal learning characteristic of the past and assume more responsibility for educating children so that they can most effectively develop their innate capacities for intelligent thought and action. His charge to educators was to help children learn by doing things with a real motive behind and a real outcome ahead—in essence, real-world problem solving (27).

Dewey's message has resonance today. The world of the twenty-first century presents a formidable array of new and complex issues. The authors focus their attention on universities, which "given their proclaimed dedication to critical intelligence and their unique constellation of resources to develop it, academics have a responsibility to help solve the problems intensified by globalization" (xi). They cite examples of commitment to local and global initiatives of community engagement in real-world problem solving. The University of Pennsylvania serves as a model for enhancing its West Philadelphia community by integrating academics in most disciplines with civic and social action. Students and faculty work in neighborhood schools and health centers. They partake in on-going research projects, and the University participates in an International Consortium for Higher Education, Civic Responsibility and Democracy that focuses on a vision of a global "Great Community" (Benson, Harkavy, and Puckett).

Advancing democratic citizenship can and should begin earlier than the college level. We cannot assume that individuals inherently know their rights, responsibilities, and roles to play. Starting from kindergarten, children need experiences in confronting real-life problems and tackling issues pertinent to their levels, and learning from adults who set examples of active engagement in their schools and communities. Ted and Nancy Sizer, in *The Students are Watching: Schools and the Moral Contract,* state, "Children need to be educated for a powerful citizenship. This involves a moral contract with our students. We insist, under the law that they become thoughtful informed citizens—we must for their benefit and ours—model such citizenship, which is accomplished through the routines, rituals, and activities of a school (xviii).

Learning the habits and skills of civil behavior are important: showing restraint, being willing to listen, showing empathy, feeling responsible for something and some people beyond oneself and one's personal coterie of friends, being nice, and getting along in one's daily interactions. One has to grapple with meanings of civil behavior. This involves more than glib catchwords like "Just Say No" or non-contextual self-esteem building activities. A curriculum rich in content teaches young people that important matters of sensitive living have everything to do with hard, substantive, and often agonizingly painful thought. This can be done (Sizer 23). "Adolescents are no different from the rest of us. They resist mandates issued from on high, and most of them won't be forced into good habits, but they are willing to talk about moral choices and they can decide that some courses of action are better than others. In fact, they are eager to come to opinions on these matters as long as they are trusted to take their time and examine their assumptions as carefully as they can." They can do this in school by considering examples that are embedded in all sorts of classes, such as literature, history, science, and art, which are interesting and nuanced and in which a human must decide between possible actions (Sizer 24). Ted Sizer describes the conversation of a student in a high school social studies class, who commented, "Americans think they have all the answers. I don't want to live in a place that's thought of as rich and powerful, especially when it's not really a democracy. I mean there are way too many poor people, and how come so many are black? Maybe I'll go live in another country where things are better." The teacher honors the student's dilemma and poses a question, which further engages the whole class. "Do you want to live in a country without problems?" How the teacher responds implies that although moral outrage is understandable in the short run, it is also honorable to work to solve a problem. Students learn by example that the process takes time. It can be partly dealt with at the moment and likely more in depth later, but the teacher listens, sympathizes, and lets the questions surface. She models behavior showing that instant resolution is not necessarily the best approach to a difficult problem (T.Sizer 2-4).

It's not a matter of "Today, we are having our Civic Education period." It's about providing a democratic ethos or climate that permeates the culture of a school. It's reflected in the way a school operates, how it's organized, and how students and staff interact. Players in the school community can be encouraged to express their opinions, engage in problem solving, and be part of the solutions. Primarily the principal sets the tone, who by leading and modeling enables teachers to take on responsibilities for professional development and even self-governance. She's the one to make student government happen, where children play out the elements of civic ed. Ted and Nancy Sizer add, "People in a school construct its values by the way they address its challenges in ordinary and extraordinary times. We've witnessed the empathic courtesy at a school assembly extended to a long-winded speaker or to a student who forgot his lines; the generous recognition by the crowds to a player on the opposing team who is injured; the gathering of student teams during a snowstorm to shovel entrances to public services and homes of the elderly" (Sizer 12).

Civic education in most schools is not required, or it may be relegated to a single high school course on U.S. government. What a missed opportunity! The Carnegie Group recommends that civic ed be an embedded part of the school experience at all levels K-12, incorporated within appropriate reading, math, and science programs. They cite examples. In science classes, students might develop projects that relate to community issues, housing needs, or healthcare concerns such as testing water or cleaning rivers and parks. In social studies classes, students can read historic documents or biographies and be encouraged to discuss them. The Carnegie Group advocates for formal instruction throughout all grade levels, using interactive methods, about the core documents of the Constitution and Bill of Rights; investigation of the processes of local, state and federal governments; voting; and U.S. history and its legal system (*CIRCLE*, sponsored by the Carnegie Corporation).

There is no one best way to provide civic education. What is important is that educators are encouraged to experiment with civic ed pedagogy and curricula that are most appropriate for their particular classrooms, schools, and the communities. Several examples of practices taking place in schools include: a weekly class meeting at the elementary level, a student government council composed of representatives from different classrooms, a grade or school-wide community service effort, mock debates during an election season, and an after-school program where "Kids for Kids" reflect on their own concerns and tackle solutions.

Current events is another way to incorporate civic ed. While not dismissing the crunch of getting so much covered during the course of a school day, I still flinch when educators don't address current events. And a discussion, whether embedded in a content area or treated separately as part of the day's activities, is appropriate for all levels K-12. It's important to have a present context for local, national, and worldwide issues that emerge or resurface. It seems so natural to weave the present with history, geography, and the understanding of others' cultures. We all need to understand better the hows and whys things happen, the nature of conflict, public policies, and discussion of strategies for resolving differences. These skills are the foundation of citizenship in our democracy.

Civic education can be exercised in partnerships between schools and their local communities. In Needham, Massachusetts, the High School Social Studies Director collaborated with the Needham League of Women Voters in a number of initiatives. During a series of AP Government classes that took place after the May exam, a League member taught advocacy skills that were applied by students, who researched issues of their choice and presented cases to a state legislator. Another collaboration, a *Birthday Packet* for eighteen year olds, is designed by the LWV Needham Civic Ed Committee and distributed by the Needham High Student Council. It offers congratulations, reminds students of their rights and responsibilities as U.S. citizens, and includes voter registration and absentee ballot information. An additional school-community partnership is community service. Whether it's implemented by an individual class or is a collective school-wide experience; whether it's voluntary vs. required (up for debate), community service outreach is appropriate for children at all levels. It's a valuable opportunity for students to begin thinking beyond themselves and taking responsibility for others' welfare. They profit directly as they learn about others and feel good about themselves. When community service is initiated by student leaders, such as the elementary team profiled under "Leadership," students become empowered.

"Schools exist for its children, but children are often seen as powerless people. They are told that they are in school not because of what they know but because of what they don't know. All over the world, powerless people lose the instinct to help because it is so rebuffed in them" (Sizer 20). Our charge is to give students every opportunity to be thoughtful citizens and decent human beings. What is clear is that civic education is a set of learned skills that can be a part of every student's school experience and practiced at every grade level.

◦◦

Workforce of the Future

Much has been made of the failure of public schools to prepare students for the world they will encounter upon leaving school. How do we interpret the public alarms from business owners, CEOs, politicians, policy makers, and the media about the "abysmal state" of our graduates? How can we ensure that students continue their studies so that they graduate from high school and then stay the course to graduate from post-secondary institutions? How do we prepare them for a world in which the only sure thing is "change" and the only sure way to succeed is to anticipate change and respond positively?

One response at federal, state, and local levels to better student achievement has been the increased attention to accountability, namely the attention to test performance of students at regular intervals. There are some positive signs of increased achievement in Language Arts and Math; efforts are underway in assessing other subject areas such as Science and Social Studies; and when tests are used for diagnostic purposes, which can lead to remediation, students and their teachers are engaged in a "win-win." Let me add a brief aside. I have some issues with extreme reliance on test performance. Briefly, scores don't necessarily reflect an individual student's or grade's progress; often they are matched with a different grade's result the next year, which may represent a very different composition of students. Often too much time is spent on how to take the tests; there are limitations on in-depth and in-breath study; and there is less attention to meeting the needs, interests, and talents of individual students.

Another response, which tends to cycle every ten years, is "Career Awareness and Exploration," which is encouraged through national programs such as "School to Work." These programs generate a lot of enthusiasm and motivation for students and have great results. Unfortunately, they tend to be inconsistent because of funding, and they are often dropped. Yet, there are thriving models where kids along the spectrum of high academic to special needs test their talents and inclinations and are exposed to potential careers through internship and community service programs. These programs utilize resources from the community, who share their experiences and expertise (refer to chapter "Beams of Light: Community: TEC Career and Instructional Team").

There are many definitions of career education. If viewed as a lifelong process that attempts to integrate academic subject matter with the world of work, it becomes less daunting. Career development, in fact, can begin at the elementary level and be integral to the learning continuum by incorporating and applying basic values such as the concept of the dignity and worthiness of work and fundamental skills such as good work and study habits as part of students' overall development and preparation. Career awareness, development, and exploration don't involve occupational commitment; rather, embedding the concept within curriculum gives children exposure to what others in the "real world" are doing and provides activities that are "real life." Randy Reilly's, 1993, "American Law" high school class is very popular with students, who participate in case studies and mock trials. Through her creation of a Law Related Education Board, practicing attorneys are involved in classrooms; and the district court and local police also contribute to the benefit of students. to the benefit of students. Evren Gunduz, 2009, gets middle school kids to ride excitedly on a homemade hovercraft down a long hallway to study one aspect of friction. Angie DiNapoli, 1998, uses a space simulation model featuring an "Astro-Saucer" space station that gets elementary students thinking and experimenting about different worlds and issues. It's interesting to note that when students are asked about their favorite school activities, they typically don't recall specific content; they recount the hands-on projects that challenged their creative and critical thinking as they worked on solutions to contemporary problems.

The role of community resources comes into play as a natural way to complement learning activities. Some teachers, at all levels K-12, poll their parents at the beginning of the school year to assess their interests, talents, and vocations to see if there's a potential match with curriculum and if parents are willing to come to the class to share their expertise. Awareness of careers becomes an extension especially when students, who are encouraged to be inquisitive, ask questions, which they develop, that involve their presenters in a meaningful dialogs: what is your job; what's the environment like; who are some of the people you work with; what skills do you need; what was your career path; would you have made any changes and why?

Integration of career awareness, development, and exploration can be revisited. Life skills are relevant in all subject areas, not limited to a "Career Education" course or a single enrichment program. Exposure in the form of a one-day Career Fair where high school students rotate to different stations to speak with people of different professions doesn't quite measure up. Life skills can be introduced, practiced, and applied in all academic areas as well as other school programs involving community service and enrichment, from sports to drama. Teachers can foster the connections.

Carol Pope in *The English Journal* summarizes five areas of proficiency that are necessary for students for the twenty-first century.

> ➤ The ability to communicate and work collaboratively: Future workers must be able to use language in a variety of contexts. Having determined the audience and the purpose of the situation, they can respond appropriately whether in written or oral form. They should be able to listen, negotiate, and compromise in language carefully selected to fit a variety of situations and a variety of audiences.
> ➤ The ability to work effectively in a multicultural society and work force: Workers need to listen, be empathic and knowledgeable of other cultures, and use language sensitively with people from cultures other than their own.

> ➤ The ability to adapt and learn new skills in a fast developing society: Future workers need to know how to learn and how to cast new light on problems and issues.
> ➤ The ability to think critically: Each person needs to bring to his/her present experiences an inquiring responsive mind that probes, sees relationships, considers alternatives, predicts, and analyzes.
> ➤ The ability to use available technology, to communicate within and across worlds: People in the workplace must be adaptable in dealing with various cultures and ideas, and they must be thinkers who care about their own learning to the point that they are constantly open to changing paradigms (Pope 38-41).

ᔕ

Leadership

Leadership matters. The school district superintendent, faced with looming budget cuts affecting class size, reduction of teachers, or elimination of programs, deals with the school board and local community. The politician, who has convinced people he's the right person to represent them, finds he must modify his platform principles due to an unexpected crisis. It is an autoworker who exercises leadership through his union, a corporate executive who responds to both shareholders as well as her employees, a scientist who leads his research team, or a housewife who takes an active role in civic matters. These individuals, in their own organizations and communities, shape public opinion, create the climate in which public opinion is formed, and determine the course of our national life. They have challenges and responsibilities. Their goal is to maximize the potential of their group. They need the capacity, vision, and skills to exercise that leadership.

How we can better prepare our future leaders invites reflection of when and where to start and who has a role in shaping them. In the schoolhouse, the future leaders are both students and teachers. Our charge as educators is to establish environments enabling them to deal effectively with conflict and change, create excited learners, demand excellence, and foster integrity.

Leadership for students can take many forms. In a class meeting at the elementary level, children can experience the give and take of opinions, question authority, and exercise leadership in classroom policy and projects. At a middle school, students might be in charge of a class or school-wide community service project of their choice, which involves planning and implementation while developing new relationships with peers and people outside of the schoolhouse. Students at the high school level, when participating in an internship or community service project, can be guided to analyze how authority is exercised and ask, "Who's in charge?" and "How do you know?" and "How effective is his/her leadership performance?" At any level, children will observe conflict and change, and they need practice in dealing with it. They will experience the satisfaction generated by stepping outside of themselves.

Within the schoolhouse, Roland Barth speaks of a "leadership culture" that can establish "teachers as owners and investors in the school rather than mere tenants." Once established, this leadership culture has implications for the classroom, school, and district. Barth suggests all teachers harbor leadership capabilities waiting to be unlocked and engaged for the good of the school. They can assume important school-wide responsibilities in such areas as choosing instructional materials, shaping curriculum, setting standards for student behavior, and designing professional development. Teachers who become leaders experience personal and professional satisfaction, a reduction in isolation, a sense of instrumentality, and new learning. Barth adds that when teachers take on important school-wide responsibilities, they take a big step in transforming the school from a "dictatorship to a democracy." The change in the leadership culture is not lost on students. Rather, a ripple effect occurs as teachers model leadership and then pass the torch by enlisting students for leadership opportunities. He notes that where decision-making and leadership are more democratic, there appears to be a correlation to higher pupil achievement and less discipline problems, which result in more high performance schools.

Barth adds that principals are the culture builders. Principals who encourage and enlist teachers' leadership leverage their own. This means setting up an environment of expectation, which needs to be articulated openly and frequently. It also involves relinquishing some responsibilities, trusting the teacher leaders in their decisions, having a variety of opportunities for matching talents of teachers and issues, supporting and recognizing them. In the process, teachers become more active learners (Barth 443-449).

Mentoring others is leadership in action. Award recipients of the Gold-in Foundation for Excellence in Education note that most often they have been inspired and empowered by mentors or colleagues. They, too, pass on this leadership attribute by sharing the wealth of what they've learned. Most have taken on student teachers for whom they model behavior, curriculum design and implementation, and class management. Often they are the core providers of professional development in their home districts, and they also extend their outreach to educators at workshops and conferences. These leaders add to an increased knowledge base of content, scope and sequence, as well as innovative practices that have proven successful.

To those educators already having a designation of "leader," and those engaged in assuming a future leadership role, Stephen Theall, 2006, a former Superintendent of Schools in Needham, Massachusetts, offers insights. He reflects on his leadership tenure as a continual growth process with successes achieved, challenges met, and in some cases challenges unresolved.

> *From my experiences, I have earned a few scars and learned many a lesson about leadership.*

> ➤ *It's all about the kids. One of the leadership challenges that we face is to be mindful of and attentive to how decisions impact the lives of our students. With so many vocal constituencies in public education today, it is easy to get sidetracked. In many instances, problems arise or conflicts develop because adult convenience or adult interest interferes with the effective and efficient delivery of instruction. As educational leaders, it is our job to divert those peripheral issues and enable decisions to be made and/or resources provided where they will have the most compelling impact on our students.*

> ➤ *You can accomplish anything if you don't care who gets the credit. As a fledgling administrator in the mid 1970s, a colleague and mentor shared that sage advice with me. I have carried his words with me throughout my career and they have significantly shaped my leadership style. I have been fortunate to be associated with many talented colleagues during my career. As we faced serious challenges, we would engage each other in provocative questioning, stretch our zones of comfort, and identify a variety of solutions. Nowhere in this process was it important to gain credit or satisfy ego. What counted and what was newsworthy was the solution, not the author. In this way, we were able to function most effectively.*

> ➤ *When you hire good people, you need to trust in them. As a supervisor, I have always believed that it was important to let your colleagues fashion their own successes. The critical act of hiring someone is implicitly and explicitly woven into the belief that they can be and will be successful in their role. As Jon Saphier would advise us concerning our students, "You can do it! This is important! I won't give up on you!" Similarly, our management beliefs should incorporate these messages into the way in which we support and mentor those in whom we entrust so much responsibility.*

> ➤ *How we behave is as important if not more important than what we believe. The acts of teaching and learning, supervising and evaluating, and leading are tremendously interpersonal acts. Success is nurtured within a framework and culture of respect, honesty, and collegiality. Each of us needs to inculcate those values*

into the many interactions we have with our students, our colleagues, and our community constituents.

➤ *Maintain focus and keep your eye on the target. As Superintendent, I have been beset by and hopefully resisted many initiatives, which may have had some intrinsic value but were not complementary to the implementation of the organizational goals and objectives to which we have all agreed. The School Committee supported deep and lasting change within our school system. As a result, we agreed to two organizational goals six years ago. These goals have remained at the core of what we do. While the objectives to reach those goals have been updated on an annual basis, the belief that substantive change requires depth and breadth has not. As a result, our effort "to implement an approach to curriculum, instruction, and assessment practices that ensures all students meet clearly defined high standards" as well as "implement and assess community and school practices that respond to the wellness needs of Needham students and staff" is deeply embedded in who we are and what we believe as a school system.*

➤ *Trust your gut, make your decision, and move forward. The immortal black baseball player Satchel Paige once said, "Don't look back; they may be gaining on you." As an educational leader, the wisdom of that advice is most helpful. In reaching decisions that are often complex, we need to make the best decisions possible given the information and resources available. This is not to suggest that decisions should not be reviewed or reversed on occasion, but that we need to trust our judgment and proceed in the best interests of our students* (Theall).

Nurturing leadership becomes an important goal. With environments that are more challenging and less predictable, we seem to encounter change as fundamental. Education appears to be in a constant state of reform; there are more state and federal mandates; and there are less human and fiscal resources. We need leaders who are authentic, distinguished by their integrity, not just their technique or style. Robert Evans notes that authentic leaders link what they think, what they seek, and what they do. They make their assumptions explicit about their goals and expectations of performance. Communication is a vital skill that encourages active listening, facilitates information sharing, and provides constructive feedback. Authentic leaders are reflective and open to new ideas. Knowing that they can't handle most tasks alone, they motivate others and share power resulting in investment of the idea or process. They identify and build on the strengths of all in the schoolhouse; and they recognize and celebrate others (Evans 19-23).

~

Raising the Bar

Students will rise to meet the challenge of high expectations. The literature is replete with examples of educators setting the bar higher and getting results that were unanticipated: the principal who establishes strict behavior codes along with a caring environment, the district superintendent who provides tutorial support for underachievers, and the classroom teacher who takes extra time to mentor students. Students in all kinds of settings—rural, inner city, suburban—can be challenged with solid support structures to achieve and aspire. This is true for the spectrum of learners, special needs to gifted students. With the current emphasis on test taking, we may sometimes miss out on meeting the individual needs, interests, and talents of our students and challenging them accordingly. Take a moment to reflect on the students with whom you interact. Might an independent study opportunity be provided for a talented student who is reading way beyond grade level, a different "Stand and Deliver" model for students who are at risk and turned off, or a different modality to engage an English language learner?

During my visit to a Goldin Foundation award recipient's inclusion kindergarten I was unable to identify which students had learning challenges. Sharon Taylor in rural Crosby, Texas, continually modifies her curriculum and provides appropriate accommodations for each student. She expects no less of her special education students than she does any of the other students in her class. As a result, unbelievable strides have been met. This stellar teacher has ways to make children shine, to think they can do things they never believed they could (see chapter "Beacons of Light: Special Learners").

In an inner city school in Dorchester Massachusetts where many families are new immigrants to the U.S. and face considerable social and economic challenges, the school serves as a home away from home for its students - a place where every child is known, acknowledged, and loved. Charles MacLaughlin constantly raises the bar for his seventh and eighth grade students. He deliberately exposes his students to "tough" authors, Shakespeare and Dickens, so that they will be prepared for high school and college, using films, plays, and field trips, to make these works more accessible. Mr. Mac focuses on real life scenarios in his classroom, and he uses every learning modality to kindle his students' thoughts and actions (see chapter "Luminaries: Legacies").

Raising the bar does not imply just ratcheting up academic scores. Other pathways can spark students to increased achievement. One area is arts education, which I feel should be kept as a priority and not regarded as an expendable frill. While the research on the academic impact of studying the arts is not consistent, there is a general consensus that "habits of mind" are being cultivated. In *The Real Benefits of Visual Arts Education*, authors Winner, Hetland, Veenema, and Sheridan, who are researchers at Project Zero at Harvard, saw other skills that were being developed by arts instruction: "persistence in tackling problems, observational acuity, expressive clarity, reflective capacity to question and judge, ability to envision alternative possibilities, and openness to exploration" (Hurlbut 12). I believe that education in the arts encompasses additional skills. The spectrum of visual arts including the performing arts, music, filmmaking, and art appreciation are all about discipline in the rigor of learning. It's about practice that builds to a level of proficiency as opposed to instant gratification. (What kid would argue that playing computer games repeatedly doesn't bring its rewards?) It's exposure to another luminous world of beauty. It's increased understanding of history and the shaping of art forms as they mirror the times. It's learning about being still and appreciating the contributions of others. It's about adding to our multi-cultural awareness and sensitivity. And it's about illuminating and celebrating individual talents.

Three Cups of Tea, a favorite book of mine, is an account of Greg Mortenson, a climber who was moved by the kindness of people in an impoverished village in mountainous Pakistan. He later returned to build and staff fifty-five schools throughout the area. The very first school was set on a site with an unimpeded view of the major mountain that would "encourage students to aim high." His philosophy is "Look what you've done for yourselves and how much <u>more</u> you can do. If you believe in yourself, you can accomplish anything." One of the small village's graduates reflected that she felt a big change in her life after attending the new school. She was empowered to start a hospital and be in charge of all the health problems of women in the region. She realized her goal of being a "very famous woman, a 'Superlady'" (Mortenson). There are many Superladies and Supermen in our schools, brilliant educators who raise expectations for themselves, their students, and colleagues and definitely impact their performances. These trailblazers must be encouraged!

Empowerment

Optimistic about the potential of humanity and how each can contribute to making the world a better place if given the opportunity and support, I think of people as gems having many facets that are capable of great brilliance. When polished, these facets shine. If kept in a drawer, jewels don't emit light. When stifled in an environment that doesn't encourage creativity or allow experimentation, people lack the power and energy to generate brightness. To think that there is the potential power of light and energy in all of our lives. The release of it could be awesome!

We've read accounts of educators who enlighten and empower young people in all sets of circumstances combining high expectations, nurturing individual talents, and continually finding ways to motivate and challenge them. I share some personal memories. I remember my advisor in graduate school who gave me the go-ahead to take a risk and pursue an independent course of study that was markedly not on the agenda. His encouragement led me to discoveries, new insights, and then practical applications in "Educating the Gifted and Talented." This professor was not someone with whom I had numerous meetings, yet I would call him a "mentor" who made a profound impact on my professional life.

As a consultant, I've worked with all levels of students, even first graders, who evidence advanced reading and comprehension skills, to tackle their own independent study projects. Instead of doing repetitive work in skills they already were proficient, the primary schoolers were empowered to pursue their own areas of interest. Their excitement was palpable! The approach was more than going to the library or to a corner to read. Students received guided instruction in study skills, and they learned how to develop projects and then share them with their classmates. More sophisticated student presentations encompassing research, critical and creative thinking, public speaking, and computer skills were developed with middle school students, who reveled in the opportunity to pursue in-depth studies of choice.

When working with a special needs youngster, who lacked self-esteem and motivation, I remembered Sylvia Ashton Warner's success in working with an aborigine population in New Zealand. To promote literacy, she encouraged children to tell their stories in their language as starting points to teaching words, not too different from the "sight vocabulary" practice used in teaching reading. I, too, used the approach in starting from a child's interest in physical movement including dance, ice skating, and gymnastics to get her motivated and active in her own learning. She really sparkled! The point was and continues to be made that there are hidden strengths and talents that can be tapped. We are capable of shining in our own ways.

So what is our role as teachers? Neil Postman, in *The End of Education*, stresses the point of having a purpose, a reason for "schooling" defined as the central institution through which the young may find reasons for continuing to educate themselves. He advances five narratives singly and in concert that act as reasons for schooling: They offer moral guidance, sense of continuity, explanation of the past, clarity to the present, and hope for the future. Postman talks about the need to commit to preservation of the planet, that human beings are stewards of the earth and that a global consciousness has the power to bind people to recognize and foster interdependence and global cooperation. As the "Earth is our spaceship," we can invent ways to engage students to care for their own schools, neighborhoods, and towns be it community service, tutoring, or beautifying our surroundings. We can build on the energy and political idealism of our youth for "benign, constructive, and humane purposes" (Postman 60-66).

As educators, we can let our students know that there is no absolute truth, dogma, or knowledge. Humans can and will make mistakes, yet they are capable of correcting them. It is acceptable to know that we don't know and cannot know the whole truth, but that we can move toward it inch by inch, discarding what is false. Postman adds, "Knowledge is a great conversation passed down from one thinker to another but modified, refined, and corrected." We can encourage arguments, the knowledge and will to participate in the great experiment. Yet, it is necessary to teach people how to argue as well as help discover what questions are worth arguing, and make sure that they know when arguments cease (Postman 132-142).

Our role is to provide ourselves and others with a comprehensive understanding of diversity, both in the human sphere and in the broader institutions. Sameness, Postman suggests, is the enemy of vitality and creativity. Stagnation is when nothing new and different comes from outside the system. Diversity doesn't mean the disintegration of standards; it's an argument for growth and malleability of standards across time and space and given form by difference of gender, religion, and other areas. To this end, we can give students cultural literacy, an understanding of where ideas came from, how we came by them, and how we might employ them in the future (Postman 76-79).

Empowerment implies power within. It is not passive; rather, it involves thinking, questioning, acting, and modifying. There is a world out there filled with challenges. We need to encourage our students to harness the power within themselves. We need to encourage our teachers to also find their power within and use it to engage their students in purposeful and thoughtful learning.

∽

Excellence and Self-Renewal

John W. Gardner, whose books including *Excellence* and *Self Renewal: The Individual and the Innovative Society* I value for their wisdom, declares that the ultimate goal of education is to cede the responsibility of pursuing education to the individual gradually and deliberately. Thus, students become the architects of their own learning. As educators, we can offer "exploration of a full range of potentialities, not left to chance but to be pursued to the end of days. The potentialities are not just skills, but the full range of capacities for sensing, wondering, learning, understanding, loving, and aspiring" (Gardner 13).

"The only society that can renew itself over a long period of time is a free society, but this offers no grounds for complacency" (Gardner 2). Our challenge, as educators, is to motivate, teach, and model how to be versatile and adaptive to change. We can teach habits of mind that will be useful in new situations: curiosity, open mindedness, objectivity, respect for evidence, and the capacities to think critically and creativity. In this way, we can empower students, be they youngsters or adults, to foster a lifelong pursuit of learning (Gardner 31).

Parker Palmer, in his book, *The Courage to Teach*, adds, "Good teaching comes in many forms, yet there is one trait that stands out. Teachers are really present; they are deeply engaged with their students and subjects. They are able to weave a complex web of connections among themselves, and their subjects, and their students so that students can learn to weave a world for themselves. It's more than methodology; these connections are made in the heart, where intellect, emotion, and spirit converge." A strong sense of personal identity infuses their work (Palmer 11).

Our Goldin Foundation educators of excellence illuminate basic qualities as human beings and teachers, which they model for others.

> ➤ Passion: They have energy; they are committed to the growth of young people; and they respect individual needs and talents.
> ➤ Knowledge: They exemplify expertise based on hands-on experience, and they demonstrate creativity and innovation in ways that that successfully impact others. They continue their own professional development
> ➤ Communication: They actively listen, model personal and character attributes, share methodologies that work, and mentor others.
> ➤ Empowerment: They encourage creativity, independence, risk taking, critical thinking, realization of individual potential; and they act as catalysts for others.

We are all learners as well as teachers. In an article, "To Teachers of Letters," Margaret Metzger, an educator and workshop presenter, notes, "What does teaching mean to you brings a clarion reply. It is passion and paradox, love and hate, routine and excitement, and it always matters." To a student teacher, she comments, "When you consider a life's work, consider not just what you will take to the task, but what it will give to you. Which job will give self-respect and challenge? Which job will give you a world of ideas? Which job will be intellectually challenging? Which job will enlarge you and give you life in abundance? Which job will give you lessons of the heart?" (Metzger 27)

ଚ୬

Reflections of the Reader

You are encouraged to continue your self-reflection. Discussions with others about topics of interest can also be constructive. *Above and Beyond: Excellence in Education* has an interactive forum for extended dialogs where you can enter your reflections and pose your questions. Go to www.goldinfoundation.org, where you can link to *Above and Beyond: Excellence in Education*. You are welcome to participate.

Rays of Sunshine

> ➤ *How might you use your sense of childhood wonder as a springboard to learning beyond elementary school?*
> ➤ *Wonder. Question. Engage. How do your classroom activities utilize these strategies?*

Special Learners:

> ➤ *Philosophically, how could you make a case that we are all special learners?*
> ➤ There continues to be a debate about the model of inclusion for all learners. Based on your philosophy, *try to envision one positive application of the inclusion model and one way that a classroom might be negatively impacted.*
> ➤ Daly and Renna's high school program, *Writing with Colors,* can be adapted for all grades. *Using one of your lessons, take a look at how the strategy might be readily incorporated.*

Community:

> ➤ *What's your take on the "imprinting" applauded by Whitman's poem?*
> ➤ *Do you think raising, teaching, and nurturing children need to be a shared responsibility?*
> ➤ "When you have a tree, you have many limbs. The balance of limbs on both sides of the tree makes it strong. Otherwise the tree might break. The limbs hold up the bloom" (Blanca Diaz, 2005).

Before making sure the limbs of your school's "tree" is balanced, it is first important to recognize just how many limbs there are to your school. So think about it. Who and what make up the "limbs" in your school? Are these limbs balanced? If so, what creates that balance? Would you consider these limbs out of balance? Why? Which areas of the school's limbs need to be pruned? Which need more nourishment in order to create the balance necessary for your school's tree to "hold the bloom?"

<u>Instruction</u>

> *How do you give purpose and relevance to your instruction?*

> *How might you frame "essential questions" that build on big ideas? Look at your curriculum units and develop several questions that get at the core of issues, problems, and concepts that also have relevance for the future.*

> *How can teachers keep gifted students engaged if they already know the "new" material being introduced to other learners?*

> Hands-on matters! Science by researching, questioning, and defending; internships that give high school kids opportunities to test their talents and interests while learning real-life skills in the working world; activities in math and other subject areas that build on real life scenarios; curriculum content areas that make connections with each other are all examples of meaningful learning. *Take a lesson unit you already have and infuse hands-on approaches.*

> From early childhood, kids show remarkable aptitude for creative play, alternative solutions to problems, and flexibility. *Using one of your established lessons, take a backwards look at it and analyze how you encourage critical and creative thinking.*

> Children can generate their own electricity. *Do you allow and encourage time and opportunity for your students:*
> *to discover?*
> *to take risks? (and make mistakes)*
> *to make personal choices of activities or materials?*

to interact with each other?
to let their ideas percolate?

Legacies:

> ➤ Legacies live. What educators of excellence have done is invite the question: *what might you do inside and outside of the classroom?*
> ➤ *What legacy were you left by an educator in your life? How does it influence your planning and delivery of instruction?*

Reflection:

> ➤ Our world demands the quick response–to the email, the fax, the standardized test. Yet, critical and creative thinkers reflect the importance of allowing time for ideas to germinate. Perhaps this involves writing down a phrase, making a quick sketch, or just time for letting thoughts enter one's consciousness. Generally, the action is revisited, perhaps many times. *How might you incorporate the strategy of waiting or allowing patience for the full response? When you ask questions of your students, can you incorporate a little silent waiting time for responses?*

Discipline:

> ➤ "Let them know you're the boss. Set the tone. Don't smile until the third week. Don't be the kids' friend." Admonitions about discipline abound. Yet, while it is important to set boundaries, there are ways to establish a classroom of democracy where codes of behavior are mutually developed by you and your students. Consistency of behavior, and dissent and difference of opinions are not only tolerated but also respected. Essentially, the Golden Rule rules: "Be good unto others…" *How might you incorporate some of the following key words: "respect, patience, tolerance, altruism, connections?"*

Rising to High Expectations:

> The inner city superintendent or principal who runs a tight ship. The teacher who sets clear boundaries for behavior and achievement, yet aims for more and better (above and beyond), encouraging students to take risks and providing enrichment opportunities. The teacher who connects personally with each student with more than a passing greeting, who refers to something happening in that student's life, writes a special note, or attends a school event. Many educators of excellence comment that education is more than the "business" of lessons or what happens during the school day. *Does this idea of a more personal interaction connect with you? How might you build this into your repertoire of teaching strategies?*

Professional Development

> Very often, it's the school principal who recognizes a need for his/her staff and then develops a teacher-training workshop. *How might school leaders coordinate professional development with their teacher partners? What do you think about the "teacher leaders" as discussed ("Leadership," "Professional Development")? Might this work in your school?*

Creating independent learners:

> *How can you pass on the challenge of learning on your own and for yourself to your students?*
> *What lesson that you already "own" could be transformed, at least in part, by including independent learning?*

Celebrating diversity:

> The United States developed as a nation of immigrants. What is somewhat unique about our nation is the remarkable array of people having different heritages and cultures and languages.

Our classrooms of today reflect more heterogeneous groups than ever, creating new and different challenges for teachers and students. At the same time, there are so many great opportunities for teaching and learning. *Using one unit, lesson, or initiative, how could you invite the "celebration of diversity?"*

➤ Recognizing and accommodating diversity in one's classroom and school is a challenge. *Why should we celebrate diversity? As a teacher, where do you start? Why could this question be the foundation of a good/necessary classroom discussion?*

☙

Bibliography

Each of the histories and her-stories has information submitted by nominators for each award recipient, which Harriet Goldin has edited. Reflections of the educators, who are profiled, are in italics.

Introduction:

Colvin, Geoffrey Sr., ed. "What It Takes to Be Great: Secrets of Greatness." *Fortune*, (October 19, 2006).

Gardner, John W. *Excellence: Can We Be Equal and Excellent Too?* New York: Harper and Row, 1961.

Goldin Foundation. <http://www.goldinfoundation.org>.

Rays of Sunshine: A Time of Wonder

Carson, Rachel. *The Sense of Wonder.* New York: Harper Collins, 1998.

Beth Altchek
Nominators:
    Kim Noltonson
    Mary Canner
    Emilee Carter Crowell
    Theresa Carter Crowell
    Karen Economopoulos
    Henry Haugland

Elaine (Lanie) Higgins
Nominators:
    Beverley Daniel
    Evander French Jr.
    Tara S. Kosinski
    Dr. Marc Kerble

Matt Torrens
Nominators:
    Jeff Anderson
    Gail Wasserman

Igniters: To Worlds Beyond

Zafon, Carlos Ruiz. *The Shadow of the Wind*. New York: Penguin, 2001.

Angela DiNapoli
Nominators:
    Dr. Laurie Sullivan
    Larry White
    Dan DeWolf
    William L. Burke III

Judi Paradis
Nominators:
    Christine Mirabito
    Antoinette Vardaro
    Patricia Ste. Marie
    Cynthia Stern
    John Barry
    Maralynn L. Johnson

Spotlights: The Whole Child:

Margolis, Elizabeth. "Letters." *Needham Times*, (March 7, 1991): 4.

Review of "No Child…" by Nilaja Sun. *Playbook: Encore, The Performing Arts*, (Nov. – Dec. 2007).

Whynott, Douglas, review of "Note by Note: A Celebration of the Piano Lesson," by Tricia Tunstall. *Boston Sunday Globe*, (May 18, 2008):D5.

Bill Horewitch
Nominators:
    Bobbie Fagan
    Justine A. White
    Cindy M. Rushing
    Quetara Randolph

Ginny Croft
Nominators:
    Susan Monaghan
    Tracy Christie
    Marcia Pepper

Ruth Mathewson
Nominators:
  Julie Migdol
  Colette Zea
  Connie Reak
  Doreen Ogata
  Lisa Sibley
  Elaine Perkins

Beacons of Light: Special Learners

Kusisto, Stephen. *Eavesdropping: A Memoir of Blindness and Listening.* New York: Norton, 2006.

The Education Cooperative (TEC). <http://www.tec-coop.org>.

Sharon Taylor
Nominators:
  Carolyn York
  Ronnie Davenport
  Vicki Randolph
  Lynda Kubin
  Jodi Lamb
  Shelley Cochran

Patrick Daly and Allison Renna
Nominators:
  Dr. Susan I. Parrella
  Thomas O'Toole
  John Graceffa

Deborah Henry
Nominators:
  George Fahey
  Dan Meyers
  Pauyl Madden
  Madelyn Moskowitz
  Ed Freedie

Leadership:

Meier, Deborah, Theodore R. Sizer, and Nancy Faust Sizer. *Keeping Schools: Letters to Families from Principals of Two Small Schools*. Boston: Beacon Press, 2004.

Mortenson, Greg and David Oliver Relin. *Three Cups of Tea*. New York: Penguin, 2006.

Peterson, Kent and Terrance Deal. "How Leaders Influence the Culture of Schools." *Educational Leadership* (September 1998): 28-30.

Gayla Haas & Kim Houser
Nominators:
   Donna Davenport
   Christy Co-Van
   Christine Maxwell
   Michael Joseph
   Christy Maxwell

Peggy Bryan
Nominators:
   Gerry Chartrand
   Teachers and staff of Sherman Oaks School

Jerry Goldberg
Nominators:
   Lynn Hunt
   Audrey Seyffert
   Kevin Crowley
   John Hughes
   Stuart Peskin
   Mary Cantor
   Joseph Ailinger
   Jean Roberts
   Don Bevilander

Beams of Light: Community

Blanca Diaz
Nominators:
- Jim Russell
- Bob Lowry
- Bryce Williamson
- Sylvia Rabago
- Juan Francisco Uribe
- Fernando and Isabel Mendoza

TEC Career & Instructional Team: Margie Glou, Fran Peters, & Judie Strauss
Nominators:
- Mary Lou Karahalis
- Ed Turley
- Harriet Goldin

The Education Cooperative (TEC). <http://www.tec-coop.org>.

Luminaries: Legacies

Clinton, Bill. *Giving: How Each of Us Can Change the World*. New York: Knopf, 2007.

Eleanor Donato
Nominators:
- James Duffy
- Brian Donato
- Pam Bourke
- Sr. Eileen Sullivan
- Kara Conceison

Dianne Langley
Nominators:
- Cynthia Crohan
- Elizabeth Ward
- Zach Galvin
- Margaret Hagemeister
- Mary Louise Carey
- Anson M. Smith

Kari-Ann Darragh
Nikoleta Papadopoulos
Matthew Brenneman

Charles MacLaughlin
Nominators:
Caitlin O'Donnell
Johanna Lynch
Rebecca Maltese
Lodia Condon
Karen Grygorcewicz
Charles Kellman
Katie Barnes
Mary Lou Amrhein
Jackie Miranda

Reflections of the Author

Reflection

Benson, Herbert. "Relaxation Response." *Benson-Henry Institute for Mind Body Medicine*, (2009), <http://www.mbmi.org>.

Friedman, Thomas. "Behind Every Grad." *New York Times*, June 10, 2005.

Power of Communication

Palmer, Parker. *The Courage to Teach*. San Francisco: Jossey-Bass, 1997.

Instruction

Fried, Robert. *The Passionate Learner*. Boston: Beacon Press, 2001.

Differentiated Instruction

Gardner, John W. *Excellence: Can We Be Equal and Excellent Too?* Revised edition. New York: Norton, 1995.

Meier, Deborah, Theodore R. Sizer, and Nancy Faust Sizer. *Keeping Schools: Letters to Families from Principals of Two Small Schools*. Boston: Beacon Press, 2004.

Critical Thinking

Bloom, B. S. *Taxonomy of Educational Objectives, Handbook I: The Cognitive Domain*. New York: David McKay, 1956.

Roso, Calvin G. "Higher-Level Tweaking." *Big Ideas Education E-Journal*, Authentic Education. (2007). <http://www.authenticeducation.org/bigideas/article.lasso?artid+79>.

Wiggins, Grant. "What Is an Essential Question?" *Big Ideas Education E-Journal*, Authentic Education. (Nov. 15, 2007). <http://www.authenticeducation.org/bigideas/article.lasso?artid=53>.

Wiggins, Grant and Jay McTighe. *Understanding by Design*. 2nd edition. New Jersey: Prentice Hall, 2005.

Creative Thinking and Problem Solving

Barbe, Walter B. and Joseph S. Renzulli, eds. *Psychology and Education of the Gifted*. New York: Irvington. 1981.

"Creative Thinking Techniques." Office of Gifted and Talented: Office of Education by The Council for Exceptional Children, 1978.

Facione, Peter. *Critical Thinking: What It Is and Why It Counts*. Association of American Colleges and Universities, Academic Press. <http://www.insightassessment.com/pdf_files/what&why2007.pdf. 1998>.

International Center for Studies in Creativity at Buffalo State University of New York. <http://www.buffalostate.edu/creativity/programs.xml>.

Parnes, Sidney J. (Ed.) *Source Book for Creative Problem Solving: A Fifty Year Digest of Proven Innovation Processes*. *Creative Education*. Foundation Amherst, MA: Creative Education Foundation, 1992.

Prince, George. "Creative Thinking." Lecture given at Synectics Inc. in Cambridge, MA, 1978.

Renzulli, Joseph S and Sally M. Reis. *The Schoolwide Enrichment Model: A Comprehensive Plan for Educational Excellence*. Mansfield Center, Connecticut: Creative Learning Press, 1985.

Sternberg, Robert and Wendy M. Williams. "Teaching for Creativity: Two Dozen Tips." Metairie, LA: Center for Development and Learning. <http://www.cdl.org/resource-library/articles/teaching_creativity.php>.

Taba, Hilda. "Learning by Discovery: Psychological and Educational Rationale" in Barbe and Renzulli, eds. *Psychology and Education of the Gifted*. New York: Irvington. 1981.

Treffinger, Donald. "Fostering Independence and Creativity." Keynote address given at Northern VA Conference on Education of the Gifted and Talented, March, 1979.

Study Skills
Meier, Deborah, Theodore R. Sizer, and Nancy Faust Sizer. *Keeping Schools: Letters to Families from Principals of Two Small Schools*. Boston: Beacon Press, 2004.

Robinson, Francis Pleasant. "SQ3R." *Effective Study*. 4th edition. New York: Harper Collins, 1970.

Mentoring

Cramer, Maria. "Disconnected." *Boston Globe*, (May 27, 2008): B1, B6.

Meier, Deborah, Theodore R. Sizer, and Nancy Faust Sizer. *Keeping Schools: Letters to Families from Principals of Two Small Schools*. Boston: Beacon Press, 2004.

Professional Development

Dunne, Faith, Bill Nave, and Anne Lewis. "Critical Friends Groups: Teachers Helping Teachers to Improve Student Learning." *Phi Delta Kappa International, 28*, (Dec. 2000):9-12.

"Critical Friends Group." Houston, Texas: *Houston A+ Challenge*. 2004.

Teacher Retention

"Dover-Sherborn Mentor Program." Dover-Sherborn School District, MA.

Honawar, Vaishali. "Teachers Tell Researchers They Like their Jobs." *Education Week*, Aug. 1, 2007, <http://*www.edweek.org/ew/contributors/ vaishali.honawar*>.

McCourt, Frank. *Teacher Man: A Memoir*. New York: Scribner, 2005.

Murray, Jake and Jim Vetter. "Social Emotional Climate of New Teachers." Lecture at Wellesley College for Women: Open Circle Program, Oct. 6, 2005.

Palmer, Kimberly. "Why Teachers Quit." *Teacher Magazine*, 18, no. 6; (May 1, 2007): 45.

Wallis, Claudia. "How To Make Great Teachers." *Time*, 171, no.8, (Feb. 25, 2008), 28-34.

Leadership

Barth, Roland. "Teacher Leader." *Phi Betta Kappa*. (Feb. 2001): 443-449.

Evans, Robert. "The Human Face of Reform." *Educational Leadership*. (Sept. 1993), 19-23.

Theall, Stephen. *Goldin Foundation Educators Forum*. Lecture on May 23, 2006.

Early Childhood Education

Griffin, Lynne Reeves. *Negotiation Generation: Take Back Your Parental Authority Without Punishment*. New York: Berkley Books, 2007.

Ostrow, Nicole. "Preschool Tied to Higher Math Skills." *The Boston Globe*, (August 29, 2008): A2.

Seidel, Steve. "Education After No Child Left Behind: A Brief Look at Boston and MA." *Playbook Encore The Performing Arts*. Boston. Nov.-Dec. 2007.

Tough, Paul. "24/7 School Reform." *New York Times Magazine*, (Sept. 7, 2008): 17-19.

Workforce of the Future

Pope, Carol A. "Our Time Has Come; English for the Twenty-First Century." *English Journal*. (March 1993): 38-41.

Civic Education

Benson, Lee, Ira Harkavy, and John Puckett. *Dewey's Dream.* Philadelphia, PA: Temple University Press, 2007.

"Civic Mission of Schools." New York: CIRCLE and Carnegie Corporation of New York, 2003, 30-32.

Sizer, Theodore R. and Nancy Faust Sizer. *The Students Are Watching: Schools and the Moral Contract.* Boston: Beacon Press, 1999.

Raising the Bar

Hurlbut, Ann Boston. "Drawing Lessons." *Boston Globe*, (April 27, 2008): 11-12.

Empowerment, Excellence, and Self-Renewal

Dunne, Faith, Bill Nave, and Anne Lewis. "Critical Friends Groups: Teachers Helping Teachers to Improve Student Learning." *Phi Delta Kappa International.* (Dec. 2000).

Gardner, John W. *Excellence: Can We Be Equal and Excellent Too?* New York: Harper and Row, 1961.

Gardner, John W. *Self Renewal: The Individual and the Innovative Society.* New York: Harper & Row, 1963.

Meier, Deborah. *In Schools We Trust: Creating Communities of Learning in an Era of Testing and Standardization.* Boston: Beacon Press, 2002.

Metzger, Margaret. "Two Teachers of Letters." *Harvard Educational Review*, 56, no. 4. (Nov. 1986):27.

Mortenson, Greg and David Oliver Relin. *Three Cups of Tea.* New York: Penguin, 2006.

Palmer, Parker. *The Courage to Teach.* San Francisco: Jossey-Bass, 1997.

Postman, Neil. *End of Education.* New York: Alfred A. Knopf, 1995.

Appendix

History of the Goldin Foundation for Excellence in Education

The Goldin Foundation for Excellence in Education was started by Harriet Goldin in 1989 with the support of her family, Marshall, Shari, and Jay Goldin. Recognizing the need to attract new teachers as well as retain quality teachers, the foundation sought a pathway to recognize and reward educators who have made outstanding contributions in their classrooms, schools, and communities. Colleagues and others in the school community reflect, nominate, and select peers who evidence this level of commitment.

The foundation recognizes achievement and fosters respect for and appreciation of educators. Validation of these "unsung heroes" provides much needed applause as well as excitement to the profession. This boosts morale in what could be solitary success in an individual classroom. Award recipients have further opportunities to "give back" to their profession by mentoring and providing professional development, all of which affect the lives of students. Targeting charitable contributions with a mission and hands-on project execution also serves as a model for other citizens who want to "make a difference."

The Goldin Foundation first established a collaboration with The Education Cooperative (TEC), a consortium of sixteen public school systems in metro-west Boston. In 2000, the Goldin Foundation replicated its successful model, with successive groups operating independently, each with its own advisory board, award recognition process, and *Goldin Foundation Educators Forum*. The Education Collaborative of Greater Boston (EDCO), serving twenty-one urban and suburban school districts in the greater Boston metropolitan area, initiated the program in 2001. In 2002, the program model expanded to school systems in the Silicon Valley, California region, now serving seventeen school districts. In 2004, the program broadened its outreach to sixteen school systems served by the Region 4 Education Service Center in Houston, Texas.

The award process includes dissemination of nomination packets to participating school systems, peer nomination, selection of recipients representing different levels, and an annual *Goldin Foundation Educators Forum* at which recipients share their projects and insights. Educators' projects are publicized by the Goldin Foundation, and there is also a continuing *Goldin Foundation Educators Network*. The latter includes forums with guest speakers and a multi-disciplinary listing describing award recipients' projects for providing professional development and/or consultation to other school systems and connecting with undergraduate and graduate students interested in becoming teachers in local colleges. Advisory boards, which are composed of representatives from different school districts and from elementary, middle school, high school, and administration levels, serve with the Goldin family. Members have been former award recipients of Excellence for Education in their communities.

Other sites may be chosen to replicate the model. The Goldin Foundation will fund each successive group of school systems for a minimum of five years. It will seek additional contributions to add to its perpetual endowment from sponsors in local communities and others interested in supporting education. In addition, the foundation is willing to mentor other community and family groups who are interested in furthering the concept.

Participating School Districts:

School districts served by The Education Cooperative (TEC)/ Metro-West Boston, Massachusetts:

Canton, Dedham, Dover, Dover-Sherborn, Framingham, Holliston, Hopkinton, Medfield, Natick, Needham, Norwood, Sherborn, The Education Cooperative, Walpole, Wayland, Wellesley, Westwood

School districts served by the Education Collaborative of Greater Boston, Inc. (EDCO), Waltham, Massachusetts:

Acton, Acton-Boxborough, Arlington, Bedford, Belmont, Boston Archdiocese, Boxborough, Brookline, Carlisle, Concord, Concord-Carlisle, Lexington, Lincoln, Lincoln-Sudbury, Manchester-Essex, Newton, Sudbury, Waltham, Watertown, Weston, Winchester

School districts served in the Silicon Valley, California region:

Cambrian, Campbell Union, Campbell Union High School, Cupertino, Fremont Union High School, Lakeside, Loma Prieta, Los Altos, Los Gatos-Saratoga High School, Los Gatos Union, Luther Burbank, Moreland, Mountain View-Los Altos Union High School, Mountain View Whisman, Saratoga Union, Sunnyvale, Union

School districts served by the Houston Region 4 Education Service Center, Houston, Texas:

Aldine ISD, Anahuac ISD, Barbers Hill ISD, Channelview ISD, Cleveland ISD, Crosby ISD, Devers ISD, East Chambers ISD, Goose Creek ISD, Hardin ISD, Huffman ISD, Hull-Daisetta ISD, Liberty ISD, Sheldon ISD, Tarkington ISD, Houston ISD Central District (Lamar High School, Lanier Middle School), Houston ISD West District (Lovett Elementary School)

☙

Goldin Foundation Educators Network

The *Goldin Foundation for Excellence Education* recognizes and rewards educators who have made outstanding contributions in their classrooms, schools, and communities. Since its inception in 1990, the foundation has sought to foster the respect for and appreciation of educators.

Goldin Foundation award recipients, who participate in the *Goldin Foundation Educators Network*, are available for consultation and professional development with other educators and school districts. They may also be available for seminars, meetings, and/or discussions with college students who are pursuing careers in education. Any consulting or professional development fees are arranged directly by the participant and host.

The interdisciplinary listing of educators notes descriptions of the projects for which they received an "Excellence in Education" award, current interests and activities, and contact information. Among the categories are *Administration, Early Childhood Education, English/Language Arts, Foreign Language, Inclusion, Leadership, Library/Information Technology, Mentoring, Social Studies, Science, and World Geography.*

Sharing best practices is a good and natural consequence of recognizing educators for "Excellence in Education." The Goldin Foundation provides annual grants for professional development utilizing award recipients, "consultants," for its member school districts. A school district can shape the opportunity to meet its needs, for example; teacher workshop, consultation with department chairs, or model lesson. Please refer to the Goldin Foundation web site *www.goldinfoundation.org* for further information about the grant process and the listing of educators: "Activities: Educators Network and Professional Development Grants" and "Educators Network." To contact a *Goldin Foundation Excellence in Education* award recipient, you may directly email, write, or call the educator; or you may email the Goldin Foundation: *harrietgoldin @yahoo.com.*

THE GOLDIN FOUNDATION
FOR EXCELLENCE IN EDUCATION

Award Recipients

The Education Cooperative

1991

Joseph Auciello, English Teacher, Wayland High School, Wayland School District

Mary Barrett, Grade 3 Teacher, Eliot School, Needham School District

Leslie Codianne, Special Education Teacher, Holliston Middle School, Holliston School District

Susan Logsdon, Grade 1 Teacher, Pine Hill School, Sherborn School District

Walter Peterson, English Teacher, Norwood High School, Norwood School District

Robin Rossi, Grade 2 Teacher, Claypit Hill School, Wayland School District

1992

Patricia Cote, Social Studies Teacher, Natick High School, Natick School District

Patricia Fountain, Grade 5 Teacher, Holliston Middle School, Holliston School District

Daniel Frio, Social Studies Teacher, Wayland High School, Wayland School District

Judith Carmody, Math Teacher, Wellesley Middle School, Wellesley School District

Helen Sagan, Music Teacher, Mitchell School, Needham, Needham School District

Anne Starek, Grade 4 Teacher, Memorial School, Natick, Natick School District

1993

Wayne Chatterton, English Teacher, Westwood High School, Westwood School District

Barbara Friedman, President, Westwood Education Foundation, Westwood

Rosemarie Greene, Grade 4 Teacher, Eliot School, Needham School District

Deborah Henry, Director, TEC Alternative High School, Regis College, Weston, The Education Cooperative

Jean Pybas, Grade 5 Teacher, Holliston Middle School, Holliston School District

Margaret Reilley, Social Studies Teacher, Norwood High School, Norwood School District

1994

Dan DeWolfe, Assistant Director, Needham Science Center, Needham School District

Ginny Gay, Physical Education Teacher, Old Post Road School, Walpole School District

Dr. N. Jerome Goldberg, Assistant Superintendent, Natick School District

Audrey Walker, Teacher Aide, Mitchell School, Needham School District

George Watson, Chair, Foreign Language Department, Walpole High School, Walpole School District

Larry White, Director, Needham Science Center, Needham School District

1995

Kevin P. Crowley, Principal, Johnson Elementary School, Natick School District

Miriam Kronish, Principal, John Eliot Elementary School, Needham School District

Thomas J. MacDonough, Social Studies Chair, Norwood High School, Norwood School District

Ariela Mahoney, Kindergarten Teacher, Mitchell School, Needham School District

Westwood High School Governance Committee, Teachers and Students, Westwood High School, Westwood School District

Jane K. Yavarow, Grade 6 Teacher, Bird Middle School, Walpole School District

1996

William Davis, Social Studies Chair, Dover-Sherborn Regional High School, Dover-Sherborn School District

Cathy Gearheart, Early Childhood Educator, Cathy's Place, Natick

Mary Lou Karahalis, Guidance Counselor, Norwood High School, Norwood School District

Kristin Nelson, Kindergarten Teacher, Hillside School, Needham School District

Stuart Peskin, Principal, Bennett-Hemenway School, Natick School District

Regina Pratt, Former Grade 1 Teacher, Johnson School, Natick School District

1997

Olya Baryski, Kindergarten Instructional Assistant, Deerfield School, Westwood School District

Donald Cannon, English Department Chair, Dover-Sherborn Regional High School, Dover-Sherborn School District

Michael Kascak, Grade 5 Teacher, Hillside School, Needham School District

Lynn Moore-Benson, French Teacher, Wellesley Middle School, Wellesley School District

Cornelia Owens, Grade 1 Teacher, Broadmeadow School, Needham School District

Margaret Rodero, Steve Tedeschi, Debbie Watters, Interactive Spanish Team, Needham School District

1998

Rhonda Conaway, Grade 4 Teacher, and *Jennifer D'Antonio,* Guidance Counselor, Johnson Elementary School, Natick School District

Ellen D. Gambardella, Dental Assisting Teacher, Minuteman Science, Technology High School, Lexington

Angela DiNapoli, Grade 5 Teacher, Newman Elementary School, Needham School District

June O'Neill and *Eleanor Giusti*, Special Education Liaisons, Hillside School, Needham School District

Audrey Seyffert, Administrator of Pupil Services, Natick School District

Lorraine Witzburg, Chair, World Languages, Dover-Sherborn Regional High School, Dover-Sherborn School District

1999

Cora Crowe, Grade 5 Teacher, John Eliot School, Needham School District
John D'Auria, Principal, Wellesley Middle School, Wellesley School District
Ricki Lombardo, Arts Department Chair, Dover-Sherborn Regional High School, Dover-Sherborn School District
Barbara Pack, Grade 4 Teacher, Pine Hill School, Sherborn School District
Danice Smith, Grade 3 Teacher, Memorial School, Natick School District
Edward Turley, Director of Guidance, Walpole High School, Walpole School District

2000

Richard DeSorgher, Social Studies Content Specialist, Medfield High School, Medfield School District
Aimee Fredette, Grade 1 Teacher, Fisher Elementary School, Walpole School District
Suzanne Gillam, Principal, Bird Middle School, Walpole School District
Audrey Michaelson-Newman, Coordinator, Children First Natick, Natick
Cathleen Shachoy, Health/Physical Education Teacher, Norwood High School, Norwood School District
Deanna Silvi, Grade 6 Teacher, Johnson Middle School, Walpole School District

2001

Marcia Berkowitz, Department Chair Student Services, Needham School District
Linda Curtis, Fran Peters, Judie Strauss, Joanne Billo, Kathy Mc-Donough, Jane Davidson, Elaine Sisler, Ellen Sherman, Margie Glou, Lauren Kracoff, Nina Greenwald, Peggy Cahill, Deborah Boisvert, TEC Career and Instructional Services, Grades K-12, The Education Cooperative, Dedham
Richard P. Grandmont, Principal, Memorial School, Natick School District
Jane Norton, English Teacher, Hopkinton High School, Hopkinton School District
Andi Paine, Teacher Assistant, Wayland Public Schools, Wayland School District
Carol Ziemian, English/Journalism Teacher, Dedham High School, Dedham School District

2002

Pauline Carey, Health Teacher, Bethany Sager **and** *Susan Woodman*, Grade 5 Teachers, Dale St. Elementary School, Medfield School District

Timothy Cornely, Principal, Miller Elementary School, Holliston School District

Jane Hawes, Media Specialist/K-12 Director, Bird Middle School, Walpole School District *Lynn Jameson*, Director, Sherborn Extended Day Program, Sherborn School District

Lyn Holzman and *Carole Lobach*, Special Education Educators, Wellesley High School, Wellesley School District

Andrea Wong, Principal, Hillside Elementary School, Needham School District

2003

Jean Brady, English Department Chair, Norwood High School, Norwood School District

Louis Dittami, Science Teacher, Dover-Sherborn Regional High School, Dover-Sherborn School District

Susan Getty, Grade 1 Teacher, Bennet-Hemenway School, Natick School District

Kathy Hart, Special Education Coordinator, Memorial School, Natick School District

Dr. George Johnson, Director of Student Development and Program Evaluation, Needham School District

Kathleen MacIvor, Assistant Principal, Old Post Road School, Walpole School District

2004

Katherine D'Addesio, Grade 4 Teacher, Mitchell School, Needham School District

Richard D'Young, Principal, Dale St. Elementary School, Medfield School District

Gerald P. Kazanjian, Music Teacher/Band Director, Holliston Middle and High School, Holliston School District

Thomas Rooney, English Teacher and Department Chair, Needham High School, Needham School District

Lynda Samp, Science Teacher, Dedham High School, Dedham School District

Jane Tuohey, Health and Physical Education Teacher, Pollard Middle School, Needham School District

2005
Susan Evans, Principal, Boyden School, Walpole School District
Patricia Fleukiger, Nurse, Eliot School, Needham and *Maureen Graham*, Nurse, Hillside School, Needham School District
Dianne Langley, Social Studies Teacher and Department Chair, Natick High School, Natick School District
Ann Malachowski, Art Teacher and Department Chair, Norwood High School, Norwood School District
Richard Weingartner, Theater Arts Teacher, Wayland High School, Wayland School District
Janet Wellock, Special Needs Teacher, Fisher School, Walpole School District

2006
Michael Alan, English Teacher, Walpole High School, Walpole School District
Beth Altchek, Grade 1-2 Teacher, Lilja School, Natick School District
Gail Duffy, English Content Specialist, Medfield High School, Medfield School District
Mary Ellen Galanis, Reading Specialist, Fisher School, Walpole School District
Janet McDermott, English Teacher, Medfield High School, Medfield School District
Stephen Theall, Superintendent, Needham School District

2007
Jennifer Eisenberg, Literary Specialist, Cameron Middle School, Framingham School District
Avalin Green, Director of Curriculum, Instruction, and Staff Development K-12, Westwood School District
Bonnie Muir, Art Teacher, Elmwood Elementary School, Hopkinton School District
Roy Sallen, ESL Teacher, Wayland School District
Gary Stockbridge, Social Studies Teacher, Medfield High School, Medfield School District
Pat Taurasi, Grade 2 Teacher, Eliot School, Needham School District

2008

Marc Banks, English Teacher, Framingham High School, Framingham School District

Cynthia Crohan, Social Studies Teacher, Natick High School, Natick School District

Meredith Faletra, Special Needs Teacher, Cameron Middle School, Framingham School District and The Education Cooperative, Dedham

Margaret Lydon, Grade 1 Teacher, Memorial School, Natick School District

Daniel O'Leary, Permanent Substitute and Computer Technology Assistant, Natick High School, Natick School District

2009

Denny Conklin, History Teacher, Framingham High School, Framingham School District

Patricia Diamond, Music Teacher, Elmwood Elementary School, Hopkinton School District

Sandra Einsel, Director of Pupil Personnel Services, Walpole School District

Evren Gunduz, Grade 8 Science Teacher, Hopkinton Middle School, Hopkinton School District

2010

Winston Blackburn, Social Studies Teacher, Natick High School, Natick School District

Joshua Bridger, Math & Science Teacher, Dover-Sherborn High School, Dover-Sherborn Regional School District

Alison Courchesne, English Teacher, Framingham High School, Framingham School District

Sara Cummins, Art Teacher, Cameron Middle School, Framingham School District

Shevon Kuznezov, Special Education Teacher, Fisher School, Walpole School District

Miranda Whitmore, English Teacher, Medfield High School, Medfield School District

Education Collaborative for Greater Boston

2002

Holly Arthur, Physical Education Teacher, Cunniff Elementary School, Watertown School District

Joanne Delaney, Special Education Coordinator, Concord-Carlisle Regional High School, Concord-Carlisle School District

Emily Gaberman , Grade 5 Teacher, John D. Runkle School, Brookline School District

Karen Girondel, French Teacher, Lexington High School, Lexington School District

Anne Mullany, Mathematics Teacher, Belmont High School, Belmont School District

Nancy Springer, Grade 4 Teacher, John D. Runkle School, Brookline School District

2003

Lucile Burt, English Teacher, Arlington High School, Arlington School District

Eleanor Demont, Grade 5 Teacher, Heath School, Brookline School District

Ronald Eckel, Principal, Israel Loring School, Sudbury School District

Carl Gersten, Math Teacher, Lincoln School, Brookline School District

Sheldon Obelsky, Social Studies Teacher, Arlington High School, Arlington School District

Alyssa Rubenstein, Grade 5 Teacher, Runkle School, Brookline School District

2004

Sharon Burr, Early Literacy Specialist, Estabrook School, Lexington School District

Mary Eich, Mathematics Coordinator, Newton School District

Marilynne Quarcoo, Principal, Cabot School, Newton School District

Dr. Robert Gracia, Guidance Counselor, Heath School, Brookline School District

Jennifer Rudolph, Social Studies Teacher, Weston Middle School, Weston School District

Constance Joy Sacca, Vice Principal, Baker School, Brookline School District

2005

Patrick Daly, English Teacher, Waltham High School, Waltham School District

Deanne Dixon, Grade 2 Teacher, Runkle School, Brookline School District

Sharon Kingsbury, Reading Specialist, Bridge School, Lexington School District

Janet Maguire, Alternative Program Coordinator, Ottoson Middle School, Arlington School District

Judy Powers and *Claire Regan*, Grade 6 Language Arts and ESL Teachers, Watertown Middle School, Watertown School District

Allison Renna, English Teacher, Waltham High School, Waltham School District

2006

Billy Harris, Teachers' Aide and Coach, Pierce School, Brookline School District

Barbara Hedges, Nurse, Runkle School, Brookline School District

Charles MacLaughlin, Grades 7-8 Teacher, St. Peter School, Dorchester, Boston Archdiocese School District

Barbara McEvoy, Grade 8 Math Teacher, Watertown Middle School, Watertown School District

Kim Roslonek, Guidance Counselor, Weston Middle School, Weston School District

2007

Eleanor Donato, Grade 6 World Geography Teacher, Watertown Middle School, Watertown School District

Vicki Ferstler, Grade 3 Teacher, Heath School, Brookline School District

Elaine Higgins, Grade 6 Science Teacher, McCall Middle School, Winchester School District

Joy Karol, English Language Learner Teacher, Bowen Elementary School, Newton School District

Robin Moriarty, Grade 2 Teacher, Cabot School, Newton School District

Judith Paradis, Media Specialist, Plympton Elementary School, Waltham School District

2008

Melissa Morabito, Grade 4 Teacher, Nixon School, Sudbury School District

2009

Ginny Carroll, Grade 3 Teacher, Pierce Elementary School, Brookline School District

Genoveva Matheus, Instructional Technology Specialist, Willard Elementary School, Concord School District

2010

Robin Cicchetti, Library Media Specialist, Concord-Carlisle High School, Concord-Carlisle Regional School District

Michael Kalkofen, Grade 7 Science Teacher, Ephraim Curtis Middle School, Sudbury School District

Lincoln-Sudbury Regional High School Wellness Department, Lincoln-Sudbury Regional High School District

Kerri Lorigan, Grade 7 Humanities Teacher, Watertown Middle School, Watertown School District

Dr. Carla Sechman, Chemistry Teacher, Concord-Carlisle High School, Concord-Carlisle Regional School District

Silicon Valley, California Collaboration

2003

Michele Avvakumovits, Peer Assistance and Review Teacher Cupertino High School, Fremont Union High School District

Kerry Mohnike, English Department Chair, Saratoga High School, Los Gatos-Saratoga High School District

Erick Porter, Grade 3-4, Teacher, Sartorette School, Cambrian School District

Sharon Smith, English Teacher and Speech Coach, Los Gatos High School, Los Gatos-Saratoga High School District

Jeneva Sneed, Grade 4 Teacher, Bagby School, Cambrian School District

Donnetta Torrecillas, Math Teacher, Branham High School, Campbell Union High School District

2004

Peggy Bryan, Principal, Sherman Oaks Community Charter School, Campbell Union School District

Misty Hartung, Special Education Teacher and Department Head, Fisher Middle School, Los Gatos Union School District

Ray Jones, Science Teacher and Department Chair, Del Mar High School, Campbell Union High School District

Tim Krieger, Science and Leadership Class Teacher, Monte Vista High School, Fremont Union High School District

Cindy Loper, Special Education Teacher, Alta Vista Elementary School, Union School District

Barry Siebenthall, History Teacher and Department Chair, Fisher Middle School, Los Gatos Union School District

2005

Blanca Diaz, Parent/Community Volunteer, Del Mar High School, Campbell Union High School District

Debbie Judge, Teacher/Peer Support Provider, Bagby Elementary School, Cambrian School District

Elizabeth Rochin, Special Education Teacher, Cupertino High School, Fremont Union High School District

Megan Senini, Grade 2 Teacher, Noddin School, Union School District

Lynn Walton, Mathematics Teacher, Westmont High School, Campbell Union High School District

2006

Mariana Alwell, Grade 4-5 Teacher, Garden Gate Elementary School, Cupertino Union School District

Philip Hernandez, Teen Director of "The Zone," Fisher Middle School, Los Gatos Union School District

Charissa Korobov, Math Teacher, Miller Middle School, Cupertino Union School District

Zachary Mandell, Life Science Teacher, Boynton High School, Campbell Union High School District

Jane Threet, Grade 1 Teacher, Alta Vista Elementary School, Union School District

Susan Tully, Kindergarten Teacher, Noddin Elementary School, Union School District

2007

Laura Coor, Grade 4 Teacher, Noddin Elementary School, Union School District

Ron Garcia, Photography and Media Productions Teacher, Prospect High School, Campbell Union High School District

Jan McAlister, Assistant Superintendent of Student Services, Cambrian School District

Ruth Mathewson, Performing Arts Teacher, Baker Elementary School, Moreland School District

Matt Torrens, Social Studies Teacher, Saratoga High School, Los Gatos-Saratoga Union High School District

Mary Pat Vargas, Grade 5 Teacher, Alta Vista Elementary School, Union School District

2008

Candy Basso, English Language Development Chair and Teacher, Del Mar High School, Campbell Union High School District

Paula Grimes, Grade 2 Teacher, Bagby School, Cambrian School District

Nicola Kennedy, French Teacher, Miller Middle School, Cupertino Union School District

Eileen Moore, Developmental Physical Education Teacher, Loma Prieta Elementary School, Loma Prieta Joint Union School District

Dawn Nelson, English Teacher, Branham High School, Campbell Union High School District

Sharon Regner, Technology and G.A.T.E. Teacher, C.T. English Middle School, Loma Prieta Joint Union School District

2009

Brian Conroy, Theater Arts Teacher, Moreland Middle School, Moreland School District

Heidi Herschbach, Grade 2 Teacher and Choral Director, Baker Elementary School, Moreland School District

2010

Cathleen Adelman, Grade 5 Teacher, Carlton Avenue School, Union School District

Michelle Balmeo, English Teacher and Journalism Adviser, Monta Vista High School, Fremont Union High School District

Carolyn Beadle, Grade 1 Teacher Alta Vista School, Union School District

Region 4 Education Service Center, Houston, Texas

2005

Bobbie Becka, Title 1 Writing Peer Facilitator, Travis Elementary School, Goose Creek CISD

Ginny Croft, Band Director, Lovett Elementary School, Houston ISD

Bobbie Fagan, Principal, Southside Primary School, Cleveland ISD

Gayla Haas, Computer Teacher, Newport Elementary School, Crosby ISD

Marilyn Hilliard, Mathematics Teacher, Crosby High School, Crosby ISD

Kim Houser, Art Teacher, Newport Elementary School, Crosby ISD

Isabel Salaiz, Secretary, Crosby Kindergarten Center, Crosby ISD

2006

Bill Horewitch, Physical Education Teacher, Southside Primary School, Cleveland ISD

Ann Jackson, English Teacher and Department Chair, Crosby High School, Crosby ISD

Peggy Richey, Parent Volunteer, San Jacinto Elementary School, Liberty ISD

Nova Stippel, Special Education Teacher, Stephen F. Austin Elementary School. Goose Creek ISD

Sharon Taylor, Kindergarten Teacher, Crosby Kindergarten, Crosby ISD

Joyce Wilson, Counselor, Crosby Middle School, Crosby ISD

2007

Jennifer Mauk, Grade 1 Teacher, Southside Primary School, Cleveland ISD

2008

Michael Joseph, Superintendent, Crosby ISD

Carol Layman, Counselor, Barbers Hill Primary School, Barbers Hill ISD

Tammy Routh, Grade 4 Teacher, Barbers Hill Elementary School, Barbers Hill ISD

Karen Walthall, Grade 4 Teacher, Newport Elementary School. Crosby ISD

2009

Timothy Meadows, Teacher and LOTC Army Instructor, Crosby Middle School, Crosby ISD

Robyn Sewell-Poutra, Title 1 Math Peer Facilitator, Travis Elementary School, Goose Creek ISD

2010

Nikki Blanchat, Dance Team Director/7th Grade Counselor Intern, Crosby Middle School, Crosby ISD

Carol Colvin, Music and Choral Teacher, Stephen F. Austin Elementary School,Goose Creek CISD

Melissa Ann Frazier, District Alternative School Program Lead Teacher, EPIC School, Barbers Hill ISD

Steven Lee Shoemaker, English Language Arts/Credit Recovery Teacher, Channelview High School, Channelview ISD

Robin Waller, Assistant Principal, Barbers Hill Kindergarten Center, Barbers Hill ISD

We Are a Success

by Robert Louis Stevenson

We are a success: When we have lived well, laughed often and loved much. When we gain the respect of intelligent people, and the love of children. When we fill a niche and accomplish a task. When we leave the world better than we found it, whether by an improved idea, a perfect poem or a rescued soul. We are successful if we never lack appreciation of earth's beauty or fail to express it. If we look for the best in others, and give the best we have.

Made in the USA
Middletown, DE
20 May 2023

31036266R00159